TO: Bar
and Tommy

Keep the good work up
or enjoying life.

I TRIED TO MAKE
A DIFFERENCE

Bill McQueen
9-22-2021

Charleston, SC
www.PalmettoPublishing.com

I Tried to Make a Difference
Copyright © 2021 by Dr. WIlliam McQueen

All rights reserved
No portion of this book may be reproduced, stored in a retrieval
system, or transmitted in any form by any means–electronic,
mechanical, photocopy, recording, or other–except for brief quotations
in printed reviews, without prior permission of the author.

First Edition

ISBN: 978-1-63837-139-7

I Tried to Make a Difference

DR. WILLIAM MCQUEEN

TABLE OF CONTENTS

Foreword

Many people pen their autobiographies to give a firsthand account of their lives and insights into the experiences that have shaped who they have come to be. Bill McQueen has done just that in this volume. He shares interesting facts of his life's story, experiences that have molded him into who he is as a person.

From the particulars of his childhood, both likes and dislikes, to some of the special events, trials, tribulations, and passions as well as his hobbies and involvement in the communities where he has lived and served, he presents an overview of his personality. More importantly he demonstrates that one does not have to be limited by one's background in seeking out success.

Over the more than four decades I have known Bill, he has been a quiet, gentle spirit, never seeking the limelight yet always striving to help his fellow man and to make the world better than he found it. Indeed, he has made a unique impact on the world just by being himself. This volume demonstrates that he is a fascinating role model, especially for African American men. And his story demonstrates that it does not matter from where you start or your circumstances—with hard work, a determined attitude, and a belief in God, there is no limit to who you can become and what you can achieve.

His life's story transcends the mere facts and allows the reader to peer into his heart and soul. Bill provides honest sentiment about his life's experience, which has universal appeal, and shows us how much he values education and how he has used it as the foundation to learn and improve himself.

This volume is also akin to a self-help book, a powerful tool when used properly. I believe it can be effective in the treatment of anxiety and depression, as well as other areas, most importantly in building hope in those who believe their circumstances will continue to dictate their destiny. It can help one to become more empowered and in control of one's life, allowing one to consider a different course to take by holding to the belief that "*I can do all things through Christ, who strengthens me.*" If one has a persistent low mood, low self-esteem, loss of interest in life and/or pervasive feelings of anxiety or fear, the stories Bill shares may be just the antidote you need to remind yourself that if he did it, then you can too because nothing is impossible if you believe!

Robert R. Jennings, EdD, MBA
Thirteenth President
Lincoln University of Pennsylvania

"Anyone who listens to my teaching and follows it is wise, like a person who builds a house on solid rock.

Though the rain comes in torrents and the floodwaters rise and the winds beat against that house, it won't collapse because it is built on bedrock.

God put several people in my life that I listened to for their wise counsel and advice, but it was Him speaking all the time"

CHAPTER 1

Aynor, South Carolina

I was born in the small town of South Carolina called Aynor. I guess that God allowed me to be born to demonstrate the fact that it doesn't matter where you started or that you have an ordinary beginning; you can still have what many would consider to be an extraordinary life, as I have. I started out there, but over ninety years I have lived in both larger and smaller cities, all of which helped to shape the person I am today. I should say all the areas, experiences, and individuals I have known have contributed to my good and awesome life's journey.

I decided to share my life's journey as a written autobiography with a specific goal in mind: *to make a difference by using my experiences as an invitation to remind the average, ordinary person how a humble background with the simplest experiences and opportunities can transform one into an extraordinary and well-rounded success story*, to describe a life well lived with a legacy of accomplishments that benefits the person, their family, and their community, thus leaving a legacy to the world at large just by virtue of having lived. (I was in the field of social work, but my last career choices led to being an educator and entrepreneur; helping others and leaving the world better than I found it ingrained in me.)

As you read my story, you will notice three themes. These three themes were instilled in me by my father, a sharecropper, carpenter, and a bricklayer, who was a simple yet wise man. Remember, it really does not matter where you started. As part of the foundation he laid for me was whatever you do, stick with it and work at it with all you have in you. Finally, do your best, and you will always have peace of mind despite the consequences. It was not always easy, nor was I always successful at first, living according to my father Dock McQueen's three part formula for good living.

You will see that I had multiple opportunities to put into practice what my father taught me and what he expected from me just by my being open to the wisdom that others helped me to learn and use. I hope to instill in others one central belief: that whoever you are and wherever you are starting from, you can have an extraordinary life. Just ask yourself, especially in the moments where you feel like giving up, if it happened for Bill McQueen, then why not for me?

If you start thinking and believing this way, you will find yourself more open to the lessons life has to teach. I like to call many of the individuals that helped me alone the way my mentors. I recognize that no one makes it on their own. If you examine my story closely, you will see that those mentors helped me to grow and thrive in ways that never would have been possible without them or without my being open to their tutelage.

I was the third of ten children born to Dock and Idell McQueen. I was born on April 21, 1931. They named me William Bryant McQueen. My first name was the same as that of the doctor who delivered me. My middle name was from my father's middle name, Bryant. They gave my father's first name, Perley (Dock was his nickname), to my oldest brother. By birth I was a "McQueen," and in Aynor, South Carolina, that had a certain amount of meaning. They decided to call me "Billy" for short.

My mother was a hardworking woman with a good head on her shoulders who spoke her mind when she had something to say; most of the time, she was right about whatever the situation happened to be. I adored, respected, and feared her. She ran the house, as well as its ten children, and set my father straight when he needed to be set straight, not often nor in front of the children, but only when her doing so would make a difference. As a strong Black woman living in the segregated

South, she knew what was possible for her, and if not for her, the children. She believed strongly in the "someday through her children" hope for each of us according to our capacity, even if it was below potential due to circumstances or lack of effort and self-application. She would listen to us and make us feel certain that everything would be okay. Her belief in us was greater than our belief in ourselves. She set a standard by which I measured women throughout my life.

When I was born in 1931 in Aynor, my mother had to work outside of the home for White people, cleaning their houses, cooking, doing their laundry, and helping to raise their children because Daddy could not get a job at the time. It was the Great Depression, and times were tough. What she made enabled us to continue to live and survive. I am not quite sure how, but we always had enough. I guess growing up that way, believing that there was enough, I made room in my mind and heart to think that the good Lord would always look out for me from my years on the farm to where we lived years beyond. These beliefs also gave me an appreciation for the value of family life, where everyone helps out and fits in. I came from a large family, whose reunions I look forward to attending every two years, and the washing and ironing that she did for White families enabled us to get by.

Even though we did not have a lot of money, we had vegetables, our own land on which to grow food and tobacco, a house, horses, mules, chickens, and hogs. Usually we could count on my father's carpentry and masonry trades to bring in a little extra money. From our garden of fresh produce, we also canned fruits and vegetables, had a place to fish (we would use salt to preserve those we caught), fruit trees, and a grapevine. We also grew a lot of sweet potatoes. We had so many that my daddy would have to build a tent for them to escape getting frostbitten. Any city dwellers who grew up in tenement housing would have considered us rich! It was a lot of hard work for us, but it was worth it and helped us out during the financially leaner times.

The service Mama provided to the White families she worked for was not free. Sometimes, they were too poor to pay her, so they gave her worn-out clothes, often too worn to wear. The exchange was not equal, but she used it as a teachable moment. She taught us never to give back something you were given. The Whites who, poor as they were, employed her just to feel better and superior to Black people but were less fortunate than us. But my family needed an income, and Mama's work provided it, and we were deeply grateful, especially at mealtimes, for the nickels and pennies that she brought home to keep us going as a family.

Since she was working outside of the home, it was my daddy's job to look after us until she came home. One time, when I was just a little boy, even before I was able to walk, Daddy was supposed to watch over me while Mama was out working. He sat me in front of a heater. Almost instantaneously I started to cry. "Hush up, boy," he said. All day long he repeated, "Billy, stop crying! Hush now." When Mama came home, she ran to me, her crying baby son, and snatched me up as fast as she could. My daddy said, "Idell, that is the most crying boy I ever tried to watch! All he did all day long was cry, cry, cry." "Dock McQueen," she exclaimed, "you burned our baby's leg by sitting him in front of that heater!" I still have that scar from the burn until this day. Daddy eventually got a job working for the WPA and brought home a good income. But even before he got that job, we never felt poor.

Sometimes I look back at my less than humble beginnings in that small town with a population of 516 during the fourth month and the twenty-first day of the Depression year of 1931, and I shake my head. Then I look forward from then to now and all that I have done and contributed, how I have lived from then to this point, and I can't help but smile and be thankful.

My mama used to always speak to me with words of hope and encouragement. She would say, "Billy, one day you are going to be something, and someday you are going to be a good husband for someone." I wondered why I was chosen and how she could even know enough to speak this into existence. I would listen to her and smile, although at first I had no idea what she was talking about and how deeply rooted her words would be in the man I would grow into. I knew she was always right, and I was grateful for the time I was able to spend with her. Years after she passed away, I mourned for her and missed her wise counsel. I will always have fond memories of the times I spent sharing her love and approval as a boy. To this day, as a grown man, I miss her counsel and moral support.

An example of how she made me, one of ten children, feel special was the love and attention I got as the baby in the family. I actually got to be the baby of the family twice. The first time was the result of natural birth order, but the second time I became the baby of the family was after my brother John Henry died shortly after he had started walking. My brothers and sisters were usually spaced out about two and a half to four years apart, but John Henry came around a year and a half after me. As a two-time baby of the family, I used to love sitting on my mama's lap and just feeling her surrounding me with love as she wrapped her arms around me. Then my brother Harold came along, and I was no longer the baby of the family. This meant less, or at least a different kind of, attention from Mama. One day I watched my mother cradling my new baby brother in her arms.

It was true—my role and position as the baby of the family had been replaced with the presence of this new baby brother. So, I wanted to know who I was now that there was a new baby boy on the scene. "Mama, I thought I was your baby?" I cried out to her, knowing that being the baby was special. With her gift of generosity of spirit and her knack for always making me feel special, she replied without skipping a beat, "Billy, you're my 'knee baby.'" "Knee baby?" I asked, wanting to know more about this new term she used to refer to me and this new familial designation in the ever competitive world of large family dynamics. "My knee baby because I can put you on my knee, and you fit there just right—and, as always, in my heart." And right then she scooped me up onto her knee. For a while I was satisfied—no longer the baby but elevated to the still important position close to Mama as her precious "knee baby." I could hold my head up and shoulders back and know that at the tender age of three and a half years old, I had a position to be proud of. Then came Frankie. Now I was two spots removed from the original center of attention grabbing position of "the baby." I asked my mother again, "Mama, who am I now?" I pleaded for another just-as-good response. "Why, Billy," she responded while eating clay like a lot of the country folk did, "You're my 'clay baby.'" She had a big, clay-filled smile. A relative who was around at the time shouted while I was trying to figure this all out, "Boy, you better go on! You ain't nobody's baby no more!" And that was that.

Perley was the oldest of us ten children, and Mama and Daddy always left him in charge of all of us when they were not there. What he said was law. If you stepped out of line or misbehaved, then he would report you to Mama and Daddy.

I always felt that he was meant to be an older brother. Throughout my early life and into my young adulthood, he was always looking out for me. He was a responsible mentor in our family, and he always seemed to make sure that I, as one of the little ones under his charge, never got lost or got off track. He was watchful, and he was always looking out for me like a guardian angel. I looked to him with respect, admiration, and appreciation for everything he did for me, in particular, making my life easier and better. He took that responsibility seriously and always seemed to know what to do, and he could always give me what I needed at the time.

Aynor, South Carolina, was not a good environment for Black education; it was better for trades and farming. Farming changed, however, after Daddy left Aynor in 1947 for Baltimore, Maryland. This was part of the Great Black Migration north in search of better opportunities. There was no longer a great need for lots of laborers as machines were being invented to do some of the labor-intensive farm functions. They were inventing and using cotton-picking, tobacco, and corn-picking machines.

Back before those machines were invented, it was kind of expected that the Black children who went to school would become farmers, so they did not need that much education. Around eighth grade many dropped out. So, Blacks typically did not go to school ten months of the year like White children; finishing high school, which at that time ended with eleventh grade, was rare, unless Blacks were going to go to college to become teachers or something similar, which was even rarer. Blacks got out in early May and did not return to school until mid- or late September, so that they could provide labor and help with the farming. It was a different environment where Whites were treated as superior and Blacks were considered to be inferior. But even during those years, all Black-White interactions did not fit this mold.

I have two distinct and significant memories about interacting with Whites as a Black boy growing up: 1) as the mail carrier's babysitter, and

2) as a tobacco-picker on a White farm. Both involved Whites, but one of the two demonstrated how racism continued to spread. I was the babysitter of the mail carrier's little boy. I kept him and played with him, and I looked after him. They treated me like one of the family. They were always super nice to me and treated me well and even let me sit at the table to dine with them. One day there was an elementary school graduation, and I was supposed to look after the little boy while everyone else got ready. The little boy I babysat was clean and all dressed up. Then, seemingly out of the clear blue, the little boy, about three years old, looked me in the eye and said, "Nigger." I scolded him and, spotting a pool of water close by, said to him, "You are not supposed to say that word to or about me. You say it again, and I'm going to put you in that water puddle over there." A few seconds passed, and looking at me with a mischievous look in his eyes, he said *"Nigger, nigger, nigger!"* At that point I scooped him up and set him in the water puddle as promised, and he cried.

When his mother came home and I told her what he had done and said, she apologized profusely, and she had to dress him up again. I was disappointed because that three-year-old little boy had probably learned the N-word from his parents using it when he was present. This is a clear example of the profound subtleties of racism that would become the norm during the years after this, and before civil rights legislation was enacted. Following integration, in public Whites might be cordial, but privately they were racist. They might smile and be polite to your face, but behind closed doors they expressed their true feelings about Blacks; by so doing, they passed this legacy of misguided assumptions of White superiority and Black inferiority onto their children, and that was how their legacy of White privilege got passed down from one generation to the next.

The other experience was more "normal" for the time: A White man asked my father if he would lend me out to pick tobacco. I had never done it at that age but went there on a Saturday night to help pick tobacco. I slept in a separate room in the house and ate separately on the porch, not at the table with them. I had no doubt about this family's feelings regarding Blacks; they made no hypocritical claims otherwise. And that's how insidious racism can be.

Before I had any jobs in my hometown, and shortly after my progression from being the two-time baby of the family, knee and clay baby, it was agreed that I would go to Pine Island, South Carolina, to live with my Aunt Daisy and her brother's daughter, Mary Lois. The adults felt it would be good for her to live with another child in the home so she could have a playmate and someone to grow up with. I guess it was also because they did not want her to be isolated or lonely, to ensure she would be socially adept. I lived with them for almost two years. This is probably why I started school late. Mama sent for me, and I returned to Aynor, to live with my own family and attend school.

From an early period, my mama and daddy were comfortable lending me out to help family members or work away from home. For example, once I was back with my family, I had the responsibility of bringing in wood (and after I was old enough, chopping it too) for the fire and the job of putting coals in the heater at the church, and at the school. I was assigned to building fire in the stove, so that when teachers and students arrived, it was warm. The other kids must have been jealous of the pennies and nickels I got for doing this, because they were always trying to scare me about being in the church alone and in the dark. "B-iii-llll-y…those ghosts of dead people are gonna come back and *get* you!" I could hear their voices in my head, especially after knowing there had been a funeral at the church on Sunday. Although kids said these things and I was scared, I did not let anyone know.

Aynor was the heart of the segregated South, and there had not been too much time in between the end of slavery and the beginning of Jim Crow laws in Southern states like South Carolina. Back then Grandpa was a connection to that awful past and a reminder of how close it was in the present day. My grandpa Solomon McQueen was born in 1846 and was a slave and lived to see slavery end. He did not speak much, in general—just smoked his pipe and sat out on his porch on his land where he was surrounded by the land his four sons and daughter had. I think he did not talk about the time of slavery because he did not want to rile us up to anger and get in trouble with White people, who still controlled things in that area.

At the time of my growing up in Aynor, Blacks had to suppress their anger so that they would be able to get along with the White people. Blacks still had to interact with Whites in order to make a living and keep themselves and their families safe from the real danger of violence and harm that White people represented. From Grandpa I learned to be strong and work hard and not think too much about the segregated South or the environment where my family lived. Although we lived in what some would call a garden of plenty—fruit trees, grapevines, and vegetables and other crops of our own—my father was a sharecropper of tobacco and had to give half of what was grown or sold to the White man who owned the land. The money from the crops on Daddy's own small farm belonged to him. This half that my father had to "share" as a sharecropper kept him and others like him aware of the socioeconomic limits that still existed after slavery.

I think my daddy was trying to instill in me the best of himself, his skills, and abilities as part of his lineage in the McQueen family, so he started me off young on my "on-the-job training" with everything he knew how to do. I had to help my father on the farm and with other tasks beyond traditional farming, such as building a bigger house for our growing family. To get this done, my father used me and said that a "dead man" could do a better job than me at raising the Sheetrock and holding it in place so he could put a nail in to hold the Sheetrock to cover the ceiling so it would be smooth enough to paint with just the two of us. He said this because he thought that even a dead man would have been better than me in terms of how little I was helping. I supported him in this construction project, and these harsh words hurt me at the time. Nevertheless, Daddy always called on me to help him. Was he grooming me to be a farmer like he was? Was this an apprenticeship of sorts, allowing me to learn all of the skills my father possessed? I am not sure.

Although things were not certain, I was recognizing more and more that school had nothing to offer me by the time I was around fourteen or fifteen. Whether it was the substandard and segregated schools I attended in Aynor and Conway, South Carolina, or the classes, like shop, where the Black students in my class had to sit quietly, could not touch any of the machinery nor use this time to study nor do homework nor talk loudly, it was clear to me that society did not want to train us to do anything that would lead to success beyond sharecropping. It was easy to give up on education that was separate but not equal at that time.

In an environment like this, our education as Black people was not encouraged. It was almost like we were being sent the message of "You're not worthy of going to the high-quality White school. It may be in your area, but you will never set foot in anything as fine in quality as this." I began to wonder if I would miss out on my purpose before I had had the chance to discover it and fulfill my dreams. I began to consider what my life could be beyond high school.

Why me? I am who I am because of the things that happened to me, as are most people. My family environment was good, positive, and loving. I had encouragement from my mother and my father. I observed my siblings and other relatives from the vantage point of a middle child. I received encouragement from people in the neighborhood too. I also made general observations as a person coming up in the thirties and forties about the economic, social, and political environment at the time.

So, this is the beginning of my story. Consider and respond to the following questions about your origins and the environment you were raised in:

1. Do you have any dreams/visions for your life? If so, what? And if not, why not? How can you achieve these dreams and visions?

2. Who can support/encourage you in your life now?

3. What is your family environment like?

4. What needs to change / stay the same, and how can you be a part of it?

5. Who around you can give you encouragement, support and/or opportunities to get you where you need to go, even if it is just to be a productive citizen of your own town?

6. What observations have you made about your background and environment in your own starting place?

7. How can you be your personal best where you are right now? My oldest sister, Nina, said that reading is "thought-giving and thought-getting." With that being said, I hope to start you on that path toward "thought" today!

The Spirit of God led
and guided me!

CHAPTER 2

Quitting School

One of my biggest regrets is that I dropped out of high school. However, it was not a quick decision. I evaluated what school was offering and compared it to what I wanted out of life and decided that school was not for me. There were several factors in my decision. I grew up on a farm and naturally worked on it as my first job. People told me how good a farmworker I was. At the time I had the vision that farming would be my life. It surrounded me and was my world. However, there was one small problem: I was still in high school. The math, English, and history they were trying to teach me seemingly had no connection to life on the farm as I saw it. I thought a high school education was a waste of time in regards to working on a farm. So I quit high school a few months after my fifteenth birthday. The law required that children go to school until age sixteen, but no one checked on this requirement with the Black children who dropped out. So, I figured that I didn't need a high school education for a career path in farming.

When I was going to school, the schools were still segregated. Just to get to high school each day required a mile long walk from my home to catch the bus and to get to Whittemore High School in Conway. Also, I did not take lunch to school, and I did not have any money to buy food. That meant that I went from early in the morning to middle to late afternoon hungry. Ever resourceful, I'd beg my classmates for peanuts or crackers.

The White high school was four to five blocks away from where I lived. It was a huge building, and being unable to attend that high school sent a message to me and other Blacks at the time:

"You're not worthy of going to that school!" The message to the White high school students then must have been something like "You are special and valued. You get to come to school in this building, where you will be able to get a fine education and graduate, ready to go into the world and be successful!"

I, as a Black student, went to high school in army barracks, which I helped build, because the Black high school burned down, but it was rebuilt after I dropped out. Additionally, I had no plans for going to college, so continuing high school seemed to be a waste of my time. Take our study hall class, for example. Before we went to shop class, we had a study period. We had to stay busy doing homework; if not, the teacher in charge would give us something to do to keep us busy. I doodled and goofed off; I did not do my homework. Next came shop class. We picked up trash and then were ordered to sit in class quietly. There was a major difference between the two. We could not do homework there, nor could we touch or use the shop equipment. Lastly, twice a week at the high school, all of the classes were invited to the auditorium for "devotion." We prayed and sang songs. I guess this was supposed to lift our spirits. If all of this was what higher education was, then I felt I had had enough of it. I did not see that farming required more education.

I was not the only one in my community who felt like dropping out of high school was an option. Lots of Blacks quit at about the same age, if not a couple of years earlier. It was the trend. Moreover, Blacks choosing not to go to school was good as far as the Whites were concerned. So, after considering all of these factors, I made the decision that would change the course of the rest of my personal and professional life. I quit high school when I was in the ninth grade, during the month of October, a few months after my fifteenth birthday. I had already started the ninth grade and only attended for a couple of months. From this point onward, after the biggest decision I had made in my life thus far, I would go on with limited choices because I only had an eighth grade education. I was not looking at the long term but was satisfied with the short term. I made my decision, and my parents, of course, wanted to talk to me about it.

We talked. I (with my eighth grade education) talked with my mama (who had a third grade education) and with my daddy (who had a sixth-grade education). I wanted to be like my daddy. He was good in math, had all kinds of important skills, like carpentry and laying brick, in addition to farming, and could usually make a living when farming and sharecropping did not demand his time. Once I told them of my decision to quit high school, they did not seem to be disappointed. Even still, they stressed the importance of school and getting an education. Most folks really wanted you to finish high school in those days. They knew the way you would be looked upon and the opportunities you'd have if you finished, despite never having gone that far in terms of education themselves. Back then a high school diploma was not a mere stepping stone to college/career and/or other trade apprenticeship/ vocational opportunities. A high school diploma was respected; it was like having a master's degree today. You knew something and were somebody if you finished high school.

The conversation I had with my parents was nothing in comparison with the one I had with my Uncle Jimmy the next day. Uncle Jimmy was married to my father's sister. Somehow the news had reached him that I had dropped out of high school. Uncle Jimmy did not share my limited vision of how much education I needed. He was my father's brother-in-law and my favorite uncle—my idol. I looked up to him, so anything he said was the gospel truth. One day, shortly after my decision to quit high school, Uncle Jimmy talked to me about it for twenty minutes. That talk with him put the fear of God in me, such that I almost changed my mind to go back to high school that very day and beat the odds and graduate, ignoring the trend among my peers to quit school. "Boy, without school, you're not going to be anything." This coming from Uncle Jimmy was especially hard to take; his one-way conversation was part tough love and part reflection of his real-life experiences. However, I was ornery and stayed out.

At the time I thought I wanted to be a farmer, but they did not teach farming or skills related to this profession in school. Both of my parents were aware that I eventually wanted to be a farmer, so my desire to enter this path probably was not a shock to them, although maybe it would have been a little disappointing, since most parents want more for their children than they had. I also was not a good student. I probably could have been a good student if I wanted to be and applied myself to learning my lessons. This was especially true with math because I was good at it. But I did not like to do school work and school did not have anything that interested me. I would not do my homework until I got on the bus headed to school, despite having time in school and at home to do it. I talked with other kids and we helped each other do the assignments. A group of us on the bus collaborated: "What did you get for this question?" Back and forth it went until we reached school while finishing the assignments together. Occasionally, some of us would sit in the back of the school bus and push the back window out so we could jump out and play hooky. We'd get raisin bread and Pepsi Cola and go to the river or just walk around, then get on the school bus that was homeward bound. We thought we were slick. One day the bus driver would not let us ride back. He set us out and said, "I'll let your parents know to pick you up here, where you got off of my school bus, since this is where we parted company." No, a high school diploma was not in the cards for me.

Uncle Jimmy's questions came at me like double-barrel bullets, starting with "Why did you quit?" I knew that no response or reason I could have offered would have been good enough for him. The now rhetorical questions came harder and faster: "What were you thinking about?" "Do you want to be in the group of people that did not finish high school and made nothing of their lives?" "Don't you want to be looked up to and make a contribution?"

Uncle Jimmy was a force to be reckoned with. He worked as a janitor at the White high school. He was a deacon in church (and church was important!). He was considered to be the Black mayor of Aynor. He was the scoutmaster in charge of my boy scout troop 181. As such, he took us on overnight camping and fishing trips and to scout conferences. He was also chairman of the board of the Allen Elementary School and provided the land for the first Black elementary school to be built in Aynor. This was a great contribution since previously the local Black church in Aynor had also been the meeting place for the elementary school. Population growth being what it was, with time more space was needed to educate Aynor's Black children.

Although he had no college education, two of his children from his first wife, my father's sister, went to and finished college. The third of his children from that union went to college, but he did not finish before he went into the army. His daughter became a teacher and taught at Aynor. His son finished college and married a young lady who became a teacher; he became a barber and owned his own business. Uncle Jimmy was looked upon as the top leader of the Black community by both Blacks and Whites. He was real light-skinned in complexion, which probably made him more acceptable to Whites.

My parents wanted to know what I wanted to do. They said that whatever I wanted to do, they would support me. Even though I had dropped out of high school, my father did not give up on me. In many ways he was my saving grace. "Billy, whatever you want to do, I will help you try to do that," my father told me. This was to be the first of many turning points that made a difference in my young life. I decided that I wanted to be a barber. I had seen a relative who was a barber with creases all the way up his pants, and he always looked clean, well-dressed, and sharp. This was reason enough for me at the time. Daddy bought clippers and scissors for me, and I started cutting Daddy's hair and did the same for others in the area. Daddy also tried to get a job for me in a barbershop. However, you had to go to barber school first, and to go to barber school, you had to be sixteen. I was fifteen at that time, and I farmed and dug ditches that year. I also had to farm until I turned sixteen so that I would not be put in jail for truancy. Sixteen was an important age because it was not only the youngest age at which you could be admitted to barber college but also the age at which you started to be considered a man. The irony of me, the high school dropout, having to go back to school after quitting was not lost.

I realize now, in hindsight, that if I had stayed in school, I probably would not have been anything because I had nothing to prove. Dropping out of high school places a stigma on you that lasts for life. I was fifteen, too young. I could not do the work that an adult was doing. I was not, therefore, worth much to the community or society. I would encourage anyone *not* to quit because you lose the opportunity to grow and develop socially with your age group, both academically and physically. At that age one is unable to visualize completely what the future might bring.

Consider the following questions:

1. Why do you think you are wasting your time in high school?

2. What can you do to make the experience a better and more valuable one?

3. How do you view your education in line with your life's vision and dreams? If you consider them aligned, why? If not, why not?

4. What older people can you talk to in your family and community environment about how high school plays a role?

I have tried to lead by being a good example!
1 Peter 5:3-4 NLT

Don't lord over the people assigned to your care, but lead them by your own good example. And when the Great Shepherd appears, you will receive a crown of never-ending glory and honor.

CHAPTER 3

Barber College

In 1947 I entered Atomic Barber College in Columbia, South Carolina. I was sixteen, and I was going to be on my own. I was leaving Aynor behind as it was going through some big changes. Whittemore High School for Black was being rebuilt after a fire. Also, Aynor had a movie theater, which was segregated by entrance, with Blacks sitting upstairs in the balcony and Whites downstairs; this marked significant technological, social, entertainment, and economic advancements in my small Southern hometown.

The trip from Aynor to Columbia felt like a big trip, and I was glad to have a friend, McKinley Burch, with me. Mack did not attend Barber College but obtained a job at a drugstore; Jack Gerold was also with us and claimed that he was there in Columbia going to high school but only stayed a month before going back home and attending Whittemore High School. All of us were from Aynor and on our first adventure of independence.

The academic schedule of barber college as a full-time student was six months, six days a week, eight hours a day, including Saturdays. When we did not have class, we would get to serve customers. There were ten to twelve chairs in the barber college. Sometimes there would be "regulars" who would ask for you by name, and sometimes there would be new clients who just wanted a haircut. Twice a day barber students had to spend one hour in a classroom, not all day cutting hair. Back then you also had to study the anatomy and physiology of the head, face, and neck. During the week we also practiced shaving. This involved learning to use and mastering using a leather strap to sharpen the razor blade.

We had to demonstrate that we could do it and shave people with the proper technique of holding our hand on the customer's skin while shaving them with a razor blade. Additionally, they taught us history, theory, and how to go through the motions with the razor and clippers and how to treat the customer according to the barber's protocol for each step of the process before we had a customer. We also shaved people and gave different facial massages, with creams and mud. Interesting but true, even though it was not a Christian/religious school per se, the first thing we had to do each day was recite a Bible verse. Most of the students at Atomic Barber College were veterans and getting a check from the armed services.

When I first started school, I managed to get a part-time job with Walgreens as a busboy and later a dishwasher. I told my father that I was going to get a part-time job after the school day ended for spending money. However, I saw the fun that the others were having not working, and

I quit. I wanted to have fun too! After all, I was sixteen years old.

I wrote my father a letter asking him to send me some money for lunch because I was starving. My father responded with a letter back that put me back in touch with reality. At the time my father had eight children. He stayed true to his word and paid for my tuition and room and board. He set me straight in the letter. "Billy, you can make it or drop out and come back here and help me out. I will also charge you rent. I have never missed a payment for your room and board and tuition even in the winter months." I told this to my schoolmates, and they agreed with my father. I was not an only child, and he had many other children he also had to support. I felt so horrible for having asked for anything in the letter to him relating to my sob story. I should have been grateful. I vowed after receiving his letter never to ask my father for anything again and to rely on myself.

All was not lost, however. One of my classmates at barber college and a veteran and noticed that I never ate lunch nor brought a lunch to school. He treated me to lunch and paid for it one time but made sure I knew that he could not do it all of the time. Some of my other buddies who attended Allen University or Benedick College were working at this White bowling alley setting pins. It did not pay much, but the tips were incredible! Also, it was after the Second World War and work was plentiful, even for Blacks. I got a job there and had spending money and enough for lunch with some left over. Not only did I learn that I had to stand on my own two feet financially thanks to my six months at Atomic Barber College, but I also learned how to save some of my money the way the other guys working at the bowling alley did. That was a very important life's lesson: to save money. The other lesson was equal to, if not greater than, this one: how to stand on your own two feet and rely on self. I might have left Aynor as a teenager, but after my six months in Columbia at Atomic Barber College, I was a young man.

During my tenure at barber college, I did not live in the dormitory. I lived in a rooming house with my friend and my cousin. We chose the rooming house so that a cousin not attending barber college could also live there and we could be around one another despite being far from home. We found the place thanks to a cab driver's suggestion and the rooming house having room for us. The rooming house was twenty blocks away from the barber college. We walked to and from school every day, rain or shine. Being away from home on our own for the first time was not without its pleasant surprises. One day my school buddy (who came with me from Aynor) and I came back home after school was out, and both of our mothers were there and surprised us! Even though we were away from home, we still needed the love of our mothers. Little did we know at the time but our mothers had told the rooming house lady to look after us and that lady stayed on us as strong as any natural mother would have.

I have some fond memories of my days at the Atomic Barber College. Before I graduated I visited a dentist for the first time in my life. At the time I had nothing but two dollars in my pocket. He charged me six dollars and told me I could pay the remaining four dollars whenever I could. When I got the bowling alley job, I saved up and paid him the balance, which made me feel good. I also had the opportunity to see Louis Jordan. I had heard about him and played his records, but I had never seen him in person. The concert was at an auditorium in Columbia. After seeing his performance, we talked about the show for a week or more.

After graduating but before I got my license as an apprentice barber, I went to Myrtle Beach and got a job on Fridays and Saturdays in the Black community. I received notice that my brother Perley was coming from Baltimore to take me to be with part of our family: Mama, Daddy, Nina, Perley, and little Bobby. My father sent for me and had a barbershop job waiting for me when I finished school. My father raised us with the idea that it was important to not only have a marketable skill but also always to have a job. Consequently, I never was without one, nor reliant on anyone to put me up because I could not pay rent, in all of my working days, until I retired at age sixty-three. When I left a job or quit a job, it was always for something better, and usually this something better was for a job that family (such as Daddy or big brother Perley) found for me in advance. I was both lucky and blessed.

My father's vision was that his children would all have a skill and could support themselves. My father talked about skills with which one could make money. While I was in barber college, my father was backing me all the way. He agreed to pay room and board and tuition. He was the kind of father everyone should have, because he did not try to make me what he was and he kept his promise of supporting me in whatever I wanted to do.

So, I ask, why not you?

1. What do you need to change to be able to support yourself in the way you would like to live?

2. What do you need to do to survive on your own?

3. Do you have any marketable skills that will support you? If not, how can you get such skills?

4. What will happen if you change nothing about your situation?

God sends people to remind us how to follow Him.

1 Corinthians 4:17 NLT
I am glad I did!

CHAPTER 4

Moving to Baltimore

Mama and Daddy decided they were going to make their home in Baltimore. Although I had only moved from Aynor to Columbia, I realized the difference between the two cities. The move within the state of South Carolina was temporary. The move from South Carolina to Baltimore, Maryland, would be permanent; Baltimore would become home, maybe even, eventually, more so than South Carolina ever was for me and others of my generation. Baltimore represented new opportunities for us as Black people. In South Baltimore, where we first moved, we discovered quickly that the better life we sought would not be found there. We discovered the infamous Baltimore rats when we moved into our house on Lee Street in South Baltimore. The rat situation was so bad, and they were everywhere despite our attempts to block them out of our living space. They were both inside and outside, in the walls and running across the bed.

After I had two or three barbershop jobs with my apprentice license, my big brother Perley helped me find a barbershop on Druid Hill Avenue that was within a closer walking distance from the family's house on Payson Street. It was in that barbershop that I first saw the teenager who would become the first woman I would marry. Working as a barber would have personal benefits and I soon discovered, but never imagined. My future wife lived across the street. She was just fifteen years old at the time. Her name was Delores Jeannette Stith, and when I met her, she was just one of the girls. For me, however, she turned out to be more than just the girl next door. She turned out to be one of my greatest mentors, responsible for making me the man I am today. Her brother, Gordon, was a shoeshine boy in the same shop where I became the owner. It was through him that I got to know her other brothers and their entire family. At the time I did not think anything special or unusual about this "girl next door" as she walked, laughed, and played on the way to and from school while I earned my living cutting hair and sometimes interacted with her brothers. We were all growing up with each other back then, and the barbershop provided a window to the world and its changes.

Although many of the Blacks above North Avenue were going to college and some even to graduate school, I, as a high school dropout but recently licensed barber and graduate of the Atomic Barber College, was quite content to work and make a living as a barber. I was young and could work long hours, which meant many customers and led to amazing opportunities. One was getting my master barber's license in Baltimore, and one was in the area of personal growth. Maybe I was on a fast track, or maybe I was lucky, but after working under another barber who mentored me for eighteen months, when I turned 18, I got my master barber's license, which I would need to manage a barbershop. Then I came to own the barbershop, whose previous owner was not a barber and had gone back into the US Air Force. He took a portion of my salary out to facilitate my paying for the barbershop, and he probably figured that I would get drafted and not come back and the shop would revert back to him. But as it worked out, he got all that I owed before that happened. When I went into the service, I set it up so that my mother got money from the shop to help her out. This was a definite benefit of ownership—that I could help my family even from far away.

The personal event was the divorce of my parents in 1950 and the fact that a mentor barber took me under his wing, even letting me live with him. While my six months in barber school taught me about being on my own and standing on my own two feet, time spent working with and living with this mentor barber forwarded my becoming and being a real adult with a man's understanding of more complex family problems. He helped me to look at the dissolution of my parents' marriage as better for them as individuals and for the family as a unit. He also set the standard by which I operated as a master barber before I got my own shop. There was even a uniform he insisted that his barbers wear: white shirt, white pants, white shoes, and black bow tie. His shop catered to a higher class of professional Black clientele, and that higher class meant he could guarantee me thirty-five dollars a week.

A few months later, after I got my own shop, the barber who mentored me asked if he could work in my barbershop. I had a chair he could have used, but I refused to share the success of my business in barbering that I owed in a large part to him, fearful that he would take over my shop and take my clients. He meant so much to me at a critical juncture of my growth and development, and I feel that I let him down. This is a profound regret for me.

Another regret I have from that time centers on Daddy getting sick and going into the hospital for two weeks. I was making a lot of money at a young age and, thanks to my life lessons in finances from the Atomic Barber College, I saved lots of it. When it was time for him to get out of the hospital, I asked the hospital officials how much his bill was, went to the bank, withdrew the money and paid his bill in full. It felt so good when I wheeled him out; I was proud of having mastered standing on my own two feet. He asked me, "Son, don't we need to see about the bill before we go?" I lied and told him, "No, sir. You have so many children that the welfare paid for the costs of your hospital stay. We can go." I never told him that I had taken care of the bill for him.

Lastly, to end on a high note, Uncle Jimmy had gone to New York City to visit his stepson, who had finished Tuskegee Institute. On his way back home, he stopped in Baltimore. I gave him, my idol, a shave in the barbershop that I owned. I guess he figured I must be doing well to own and operate my own shop at the tender age of nineteen. I felt pride and joy. I was blessed and lucky enough to be able to demonstrate at a young age that I could take care of myself and have enough to help take care of my family as a successful and thriving small business owner!

In moving North, my family, like many other Black families at that time, was part of the Great Migration of Southern Blacks. Due to the introduction of technology, the need for farm laborers was declining. So, Daddy had found us a house in Baltimore, and after two or three months we all moved in.

In terms of owning my own barbershop: I was prepared because I had my master barber's license. This was necessary to be in charge of a barbershop. So, I was able to take advantage of the opportunity. Not only did I accept the opportunity, but I was also open to it. I had a strong work ethic and kept the shop open Monday through Thursday from 7:30 a.m. to 8:00 p.m. and on Fridays and Saturdays from 7:30 a.m. until 11:00 p.m. I also put everything into the business to make it work. The owner chose me. I was only there three or four months before he returned to the service. He saw my work ethic. I had the requisite skills and was always busy. The guy who sold it did not have the credentials; he was not even a barber but rather just trying to be a businessman and had a bowling alley underneath the shop. But all in all, it was not just luck. Luck can get you the opportunity, but luck won't make you successful in the long term.

Why not you?

1. Do you believe you could do what you desire in life?
2. Do you have a dream/vision of something bigger and better?
3. How are you preparing yourself?
4. Are you putting forth effort to achieve your dreams?

*Leading is not about the
leader, but the people who
are following you.
I realized that I could not impart
what I did not have, and I could
not teach what I had
not learned.
I learned a lot of good lessons
and I have tried to pass them on!*

CHAPTER 5

The Air Force

It might not seem logical, but I look back over my life and believe more strongly than ever that God must have a plan for everyone's life. As you will see, God was still working with me to reach my potential no matter what.

A clear example of this was my armed service experience. I was drafted into the US Army, but I chose the US Air Force. How did this happen? Well, like most young people around that time, I was drafted, and especially with the Korean War going on, I was afraid I would be killed.

I reported, and like many of the others, I took the physical exam and written test for the army and passed. But something special happened, and that was truly the turning point of my whole life. A small group of about twenty to twenty-five of us who passed were set aside and offered the opportunity to go in any branch we wanted. This was different and rare. I remember that day because there were several streetcars of guys from different "local boards" who did not get this opportunity. One of the recruiters addressed this select group I was now a part of by saying, "You guys are fortunate. You have a choice to make. However, if you do not pick your branch of service today, you will be inducted into the army or the marines within two or three weeks. Both branches will train you to do the same thing. You will be trained to kill people and try to stop people from killing you and others. You will serve for twenty-two months if you take this route and do not volunteer. But if you volunteer and happen to choose the US Navy or the US Air Force, you will serve four years active duty and four years reserve duty."

I was twenty at the time and had never made a life-changing decision of that magnitude. I thought about the four years I would be away from my business and how my barber skills would fade away. I was mesmerized and frustrated. I was not without help or influence in making my decision that day, however. God sent me help. There was a guy who had just started teaching sitting beside me. He had gotten a deferment to go to college.

Desperate for guidance, I reached out and asked him what he was going to do. He responded, "Man, I know one thing: I'm not going to be shooting or killing, that's for sure. I'm going to join the air force." So, more than satisfied with that rationale, I did what he did. That day I took an oath that I would go in the US Air Force. I was not wild about the eight years of service, but at least I would have a greater chance of still being alive at the end of the four years of active duty and four years of reserve duty. As a young person, eight years of anything, after job-hopping barber jobs and having just recently moved from Aynor, South Carolina, to Baltimore, Maryland, seemed like forever.

I got on the train bound for Sampson Air Force Base in Geneva, New York. Getting used to new things started immediately. The first night for dinner, while still on the train, they served chicken and vegetables. I did not eat chicken. I guess growing up as a farm boy and having seen chickens killed and hearing my mama talk about how filthy they were had made me lose my taste for it. A big guy on the train seemed to be enjoying his chicken, so I asked him, "Hey, I don't eat chicken. Can I trade you my chicken for your vegetables?"

"Nah, no way, man." he said between mouthfuls, "I eat everything. If you want to give me your chicken, I will eat that, too, but I won't give you any of my vegetables."

That was not the exact response I was seeking from him. I tried begging and appealing to him from one hungry Black brother to another. "Please, I'm hungry," I said.

"*No!* No deal," he barked back at me, case closed. That day I ate chicken for the first time and learned to appreciate it and eventually like it.

I was going to have to make the best of my eight years in the US Air Force. It started with eating chicken and continued with basic training. Some lessons made me feel like I did not really have much of a choice, and like with the chicken, I accepted what was served to me. At basic training there were more tests. I wanted to be a pilot since I was in the air force now. However, this dream would not be actualized. They told me I could not be a pilot because I had not finished high school or scored well enough on any of the multiple tests I had taken during basic training. They sent me to DC's Bowling Air Base as "unassigned" to try to figure out what to do with me and where I would fit in the air force. It was there that I met a White staff sergeant in career guidance who changed my life. He found out I had not graduated high school. All the positions

I had qualified for based on my test scores I rejected because they would have required me to get additional training and I did not want to go to school.

When I told the staff sergeant this, he set aside race, rank, and reason and told me, "Airman, nowhere in the air force will you get anywhere without a high school degree." He must not have thought that he was getting through to me how serious he was about this matter. He broadened his explanation to drive home how important high school was for me. "You will not get anywhere in the *world* without a high school degree and more 'red brick housing' [his term for school training and schooling]." He told me he would put me in a job so that I could work and study during the day and attend night school to get my high school education. So, I was assigned to the fire department to work in crash rescue and structural firefighting, where I rescued people from planes and buildings and put out fires. He explained that not a lot went on in the fire department, so I would have time to study and they would let me off each evening in time to go to my night school classes. The priority of this assignment was to save lives and not be careless in doing one's job.

Before being assigned to a work shift, I had to go through a firefighter training course. The assistant fire chief trained the new firefighters. One of the first things we studied was the triangle of fire, which includes oxygen, heat, and fuel. The fourth element is the chemical reaction. We learned that if you take any of these elements away, you will not have a fire. The training also included structural firefighting, crash firefighting, putting on and wearing firefighting gear, climbing ladders, riding on fire trucks, using fire hoses, rescuing people from houses, offices and airplanes, applying first aid, operating the switchboard in the fire department, fire prevention and fire inspection. Our overall goal was to save lives and property. Even today I remember some of the training we were exposed to back in 1952.

I learned once in Japan that my APO number was 994 at Johnson Air Force Base. I would be twenty to twenty-five miles outside of Tokyo. I was elated and ready to settle into my life in the air force. The Japanese handled structural (building) fires and the GIs handled crash fires and rescue. I was taught to radio and request permission to cross the area where planes would land. One night, when I arrived at the runway in the truck, when I was supposed to relieve a sergeant and his crew on the truck around 3:00 a.m., I was asleep when a Japanese driver of the fire truck tried to wake me up. When he stopped at the runway, the Japanese driver, wanting permission to cross, asked me, "*Daijobi?*" I was still half asleep, but radioed to the control tower, who told me to stand by. "*Daijobi, daijobi,*" I said, without waiting and then falling back to sleep. Instantly, I realized my mistake when a sergeant I was scheduled to relieve came in and shook and shouted at me, "McQueen! Do you realize that you could have gotten us all killed? I should put you in jail!" I begged and pleaded with him and was sorely sorry for my mistake.

As far as education went, my time in the air force marked the third significant time when someone told me to go back to school. I guess the third time was the charm because this time I went back to school. The first time was with Uncle Jimmy. The second time was from a barbershop customer who asked if I had graduated high school. "How old are you, boy?" the customer asked me. "Seventeen," I replied, a little bit fearful of why he was asking me this, concerned that he might not want me to cut his hair if he found out. "Boy, you ought to be in school!" At that time and that age, I did not want to go to school and have people see me trying to be like an adult by day as a barber and reverting to being a kid by night in school. Both the first time and the second time, I almost wanted to go back to school. The third time, in the air force's career guidance department, inspired by the White staff sergeant's strong encouragement and after having taken stock of my limited options over the next eight years in service, I went back to school.

Early discharge came and went for me. I had committed myself to passing my time in the air force because I was on fire for education. I took classes and studied for the GED, thanks to a White female schoolteacher who suggested that I go for the GED instead of a high school diploma, which would take longer. I took advantage of the whole building they had on base for education in Japan. The fire department continued to let me off to take courses day or night, but the major in charge of this plan for me would not let me out because of education.

Once they told me I needed an education, I was on a track to get educated and take advantage of all the opportunities available for me to do so. I especially wanted to improve my sixth-grade education level in English. I felt disappointed and bad about the fact that I had finished the eighth grade and was scoring at a level two grades lower. Each time I got a certificate, the major, who was the commander of our squadron, got it. When I had the opportunity to get out of service, he told me I could not leave. "Airman, you will surpass my rank of major, or even get to colonel. I came into the army air corps before World War Two with a sixth-grade education. You're starting early and you are on your way to making a career out of it!"

A career in the US Air Force? When looking for a place I could spend my one remaining year of active duty, I put in a request to be as close to Baltimore as I could. I had a survival instinct: I wanted to live just like the Black male teacher who was in my group, and the air force offered more opportunities that I wanted and needed. I was open to another possibility, twenty-two months in the army with possible death versus our years in the air force plus four years in the reserves—and life. I took numerous tests to determine where and how I would best fit in terms of vocation in the air force. I was of age to be drafted, and the draft was part of US history. I learned fast that very few jobs in the air force were possible without more training or education.

What is your status?

1. Are you of the age to go into the military (eighteen to thirty-five)?
2. Are you facing choices?
3. Do you want to make the military experience a part of your life?
4. Are you fit to serve—mentally, physically, academically?
5. Can you apply military experience principles to your civilian life?

A person who is put in charge must be faithful.
1 Corinthians 4:1-4 NLT

Through it all, I have tried to be faithful!

CHAPTER 6

After the Air Force

Dover, Delaware, was where I spent my last year in the air force. I had put a request in to be as close to Baltimore as I possibly could. Remember, Baltimore was home after my family left South Carolina, and I wanted to be as close to them for their love and support as I could. When I first got back from Japan, I went to Baltimore, and I surprised Jeannette, who became my first wife. This was a practice of mine: whenever I came home to Baltimore, I always stopped by to see her. Before that we were just "pen pals'' but not dating during the time I was on the air base in Japan. On that first visit, she didn't even know that I was back in the States. Then things kind of took a natural course. While at Dover Air Base, I continued to contact Jeannette, and we started dating.

I would go to Baltimore every week or two to see her and my family. Not only did I get to know her during those visits, but I also got to know her whole family, especially her siblings—Emory, Basil, Gordon, Irma, and Virginia. I sold the barbershop I owned while we were dating. She even went with me to collect the money.

Jeannette had attended school at Cortez Peters Business Academy. In the first two to three months after we met, she got a good job at Western Electric. With Jeannette working at Western Electric, this put us right down the street from each other because I was working for the Chevrolet plant. Things went well during that time, and we had planned before I was discharged from the air force on October 31 to get married. We got engaged three or months before we got married on December 10, 1955. I was twenty-four, and she was twenty-one. She and I had communicated periodically while I was in Japan, and while on leave just before going to Japan, I remember that she sold me a subscription in her high school yearbook. She was scheduled to graduate from high school six months after I was in the Far East. Our families were neighbors. My family lived only three blocks away from where her family resided, in the 1900 block of Bentalou Street. My family lived in the 1900 block of Payson Street, a genuinely nice neighborhood in those days.

I remember all the qualities that made her stand out as an ideal helpmate for me. She wrote to me and stayed in contact while I was in the air force in Japan. She influenced me on where to go to school after being discharged from the air force (Cortez Peters School) to pursue training in business administration, as opposed to going to Delaware University to become a preacher. In fact, she told me if I became a preacher, she would not be my girlfriend or wife. Likewise, she helped me to consider whether to go to school full-time or part-time. We had a lot of discussions about my higher educational goals. We finally agreed that I should follow my dreams and she would support me in whatever way she could. She was also agreeable to my pursuing a career with the United Way, which meant moving from Baltimore, where she had grown up and lived all her life.

She gave up a good job with the Western Electric Company to go to college to help me develop and follow my career dreams. Furthermore, she gave up a teaching career and working on her master's degree in education to have our child. She donated her time and talent to staying at home and raising our daughter while I did what was needed to progress in my career at United Way. She excelled in adjusting to five different states as we followed my career pursuits with United Way and she interacted with various social, educational, and economic groups as we moved and adjusted to new cultures, various groups, and the new neighborhoods that we relocated to every few years. She went back to work at a highly skilled and good-paying job that helped us to buy and pay off our first home during our first seven years of marriage. Additionally, she allowed me to work a full-time job and go to school while she worked a different shift, which did not give us much time together. She developed a special relationship with my family. She encouraged her family and mine to encourage me to work hard toward achieving my and our dreams. Ultimately, she did not question or disagree with me on what I needed to do to enhance my career opportunities.

Jeannette had many fine qualities that made her stand out to me as someone that I wanted to date and eventually marry. Above all, she was supportive, encouraging, generous, self-sacrificing, and very loving. However, she was not a good cook. I did not discover how true this was until about two weeks after we had gotten married. When we got married, we found an apartment about a block away from where her family lived on Bentalou Street. We got it and furnished it before we married. The most prominent memory

I had of our early newlywed days was our first Christmas. We invited two of her brothers to dinner. This included Emory, who was home from the navy, and her baby brother Gordon, a professional cook. I remember the turkey Jeannette cooked was a beautiful golden brown. I asked, "Gordon, would you please carve the meat for us?" He agreed. But when Gordon cut into turkey, it was not done. It was raw inside! Jeannette did not understand how this could be. "I cooked it fifteen minutes!" she said. There would be no turkey for that Christmas dinner. Gordon took frozen meat out of the refrigerator, and we had that for our Christmas dinner.

We were two weeks married, and I still could not get over the fact that I had not known she did not know how to cook. It had been her sister Virginia who had been cooking the meals the whole time whenever they invited me to eat with them. I was not a cook either. However, out of necessity, I learned from my big sister Nina all the basics of cooking, and my brother Perley also coached me. I remember how, in those early days of wedded bliss, Jeannette would get a cocktail and say, "Wow, Bill, that certainly smells good! What's cooking?" These words of praise were a smart tactic on her part since she did not like to cook.

Why me? I did not have a girlfriend when I went to Japan. We had no real reason to communicate. We were both in the same neighborhood. My family lived three blocks away from hers. She was not married. She did not have a regular boyfriend. Most of all, my mama told me I would be a good husband, but my mama did not like the Japanese (she called them "Japs"), so marrying a Japanese girl was out of the question.

There were several questions that I had to ask and answer for myself as a result of contemplating marriage. Among these were the following:

1. Do you have expectations or standards for who you would want to marry?

2. Is there someone whose opinion you value in terms of people you are dating seriously or considering for marriage?

3. Can you identify two to five people that you can run things by and get honest

feedback from regarding both major and minor decisions in your life?

4. Are your future goals in sync as a couple?
5. Is this person healthy (socially, economically, psychologically, financially, spiritually, etc.)?
6. Do you have common interests?

Those months leading up to our marriage were filled with activity. The last day of October 1955, I received my air force separation papers at Dover Air Force Base. It would take four more years in the reserves before my actual discharge from the air force. Perley got me a job with the Chevrolet plant and had it waiting for me before I even got out of the air force. I drove down from Dover Air Base and punched a clock that same day at 4:00 p.m. I started working there, then I was laid off two and a half months later.

While I was at the plant, I worked fast with wires and was given more work. The other side of the car had the same task. The older, more experienced workers at the plant said that I was making them look bad. I learned a real-world life lesson that day, and after I checked it out with my big brother Perley, I realized that you do not work as fast as you can; you just do enough to keep the boss off you. This seemed counterintuitive after my years in the military, but I wanted to get along with my coworkers, so I adjusted to the unwritten peer rules of the workplace.

After all, I was part of a network that included an older brother and a family looking out for me, as well as a fairly good economy. There was also favorable treatment for veterans. I also had a good track record before and during my air force service, having been known as a doer and achiever, having met my service obligations to the country.

What about you?

1. Do you have a network of family, friends, counselors, and on that can help you transition at critical junctures in your life?

2. What kind of experience do you bring to the table?

3. Can you demonstrate something that you successfully completed over time: work,

education, or experience from your background where a long-term commitment was required?

4. Are there job opportunities available in your skill area?

5. What fields are the hot jobs for your background, experience, and education in the near future, and how can you use your network to get into them?

The Monday after the weekend I was laid off from the Chevrolet plant, I applied to and joined the Baltimore Transit Company. This job would turn out to be the ideal thing. First, that weekend is the longest I have ever been without a job. Working at the transit company was ideal because I was able to schedule work around my school schedule. All in all the transit company was key to my academic formation.

I looked for a job with a goal in mind. This required me to ask myself, *Can I work and go to school and have a flexible schedule?* They provided great training over the course of the first thirty days on the job. I had a good driving record / MVR and I knew how to drive. I had good inter-personal skills for dealing with complaints and passengers. The uniform had almost the same effect as the air force's, in that people respected you while you were in it. Additionally, I was highly trustworthy; I was skilled in making changes and able to handle the cash bank they gave and not come up short. Lastly, but also importantly, the buses and trolleys had to run regardless of the weather, and one was expected to be at work.

Questions to ponder:

1. Have you ever considered taking a job for what it can do for you besides money?
2. How can the job you want meet your needs?
3. What soft skills do you bring to the table aside from what is required to do the job?
4. Are you trustworthy with small and big things?
5. Are you dependable in meeting demands?
   - Show up for work consistently
   - Meet a schedule
   - Make deadlines

I attended The Cortez Peters School from September 1956 to May 1958. It took two years in their full-time program to acquire the clerical and secretarial skills that were in such demand at that time. I worked the night shift at the transit company from 4:00 p.m. to 1:00 a.m. This left me free during the day to go to school, which took place from 9:00 a.m. to 2:30 p.m. and enabled me to take classes on their full-time schedule. I was primed for school and work thanks to my service in the air force. The Cortez Peters School did not lead to any class credit or a degree but it prepared students to get a federal job or a job in a business. But for me, Cortez Peters was an opportunity to prove to myself that I could handle college-level work.

Although I attended the Cortez Peters Business School for two years, this never would have been possible for me without the mentorship of an air force sergeant who got me to commit to school, period. Yes, I knew people who were in college, but I never thought I would go. For that reason I chose a two-year business college that taught basic skills: English, typing, filing, business law, mathematics, and world geography. Cortez Peters also had a good reputation for its graduates being able to get a job. It produced lots of government workers. I went there because I did not think I could go to a traditional four-year college.

The air force made me want an education. I went about it in small steps via a two-year business school. The GI Bill paid for veterans of the military to go to school, and my first wife also motivated me a lot. I worked as a bus and trackless trolley driver while going to school. Lastly, I was motivated by the personal reason of wanting to demonstrate that I could do college-level work.

Questions?

1. Have you considered going to a community college or a two-year school as an alternative to or precursor to college?
2. Is school/education in your future?
3. Are you willing to work and go to school?
4. What advantages does having an advanced education or an associate's degree hold for you?

5. What would the results be of increasing your educational level?

6. How can you search out the experiences with the best reputation and career-building effect for your life?

Then came the Baltimore College of Commerce in September 1958. I had finished Cortez Peters. I was able to type sixty words per minute. I had learned how to study, or so I thought. Also, I thought I had learned pretty good English. While at Cortez Peters, I had learned lots of law because the instructor was a lawyer, the dean, and a city council member. So, I was confident that I now had a good educational foundation. After I finished Cortez Peters in May 1958, I attended the Baltimore College of Commerce and finished in May 1965. It took me six and a half years to get through it, even though I attended almost every semester. I got sick and had to take one semester off. The road to college was not a simple and easy one, but I was determined to complete what I started.

I basically went to Baltimore College of Commerce because my brother-in-law Freddy had gone there. To study there required a GED or high school diploma. I had gotten my GED in the air force, but in service they had a lower standard than the state of Maryland. Maryland required a 45. Delaware only required a 35. I had a 43 on one course out of five, the literature course; on everything else I scored a 45 or above. Despite this, I did not score high enough to average 50, the requirement. So, I had to make peace with the fact that in Maryland one had to have a 45 in each area or an average of 50. The Baltimore College of Commerce accepted me on a trial basis with no credit until I passed the GED with a 45 in literature. However, Baltimore College of Commerce was not my first stop after Cortez Peters.

After Cortez Peters Business Academy, I was referred to Baltimore Junior College for a high school English course during the summer. I was referred specifically to Baltimore Institute. However, the Baltimore Institute would not accept me. I started college first as a special student receiving no credits until I took a high school GED test and passed it in literature. My mama had high school literature books that the family she worked for was throwing out, and while I was on the bus and had ten or fifteen minutes recovery at the end of the line, I read those books. Most of the literature test I had to pass came from those books! Yet another example of a person and/or situation helping me out in my life.

Second, the college I wound up at was not my first choice. I wanted to attend Morgan State. They said no. I wanted to attend my wife's college, Coppin State, and they said no and encouraged me to keep driving the bus because this was a "good job." My brother-in-law Freddy referred me to Baltimore College of Commerce, his college. I had half of my GI Bill left.

Third, I had academic challenges related to my course of study. I had trouble with the accounting course and almost quit college and would have had it not been for my brother-in-law

Freddy teaching me how not to make mistakes in accounting. My wife and her sister Virginia, Freddy's wife, kept me on track for pursuing my degree. Nevertheless, I decided that accounting was not for me and transferred to a business administration and management major.

Another challenge was one that would scare me for life: English. My English 101 instructor in college wrote on one of my papers, "With a lot of work you can be an *okay* writer, but you will never be a *good* writer." He also identified several errors that he called "gross illiteracies" on my first paper. Those statements haunted me for the rest of my life, and I never have had confidence in my writing.

I felt I could do the work based on what I demonstrated at Cortez Peters. I wanted to be one of the people who demonstrated I could go to school in the newly integrated setting. I wanted to increase my educational skills and move beyond junior college. I knew someone who went there. The school was downtown and in the heart of everything. They had day and night classes.

Some classes were seminars and met just once a week; all of this was convenient for my bus driver's schedule.

Jeannette tried to get me to go to school full-time and not work so that I could get done with school faster. Although just a young man, I lived by a code that until I lived the experience of marriage, I would not know what I had within me. In this case it had to do with being a good husband and living up to the standards my mother had spoken into me. I would be called upon to live up to being a good husband, a quality she placed on my destiny as a boy growing up. "Billy, you are going to make a good husband someday," my mama would tell me, and she told me this repeatedly.

As a boy growing up, I was not always certain of what went into fulfilling that role, but as I aged from boy to adolescent to young man, I knew that I never wanted to let my mama down in any area, but especially that one, which she had stressed as so important. A husband was a breadwinner, not a student without a job. I think that

Jeannette understood that and was just trying to help make it easier on me and us. However, after that critical moment early in our marriage, throughout my working career, we discussed her questions and doubts and resolved all her concerns and issues with respect to my professional career path or any of my choices related to work. Right then my life was as a part-time college student and a full-time bus driver, and the transit company was helping me to provide for us, as a good husband should.

The transit company had a thirty-day training period. Before I had the experience of driving on my own, the transit company closed due to its union wanting more money for the drivers. Instead of walking the picket line, I got a job driving a yellow cab, then went back to the transit company once the union had reached an agreement with the company. I remember my "temporary" boss with the yellow cab company not being pleased at all when I told him that I would not be returning and explained to him my reason why.

I was not getting paid with the transit company yet because I had not been on the job long enough to join the union. I started with the transit company as "extra." This meant that I was not assigned a regular time to come to work or a regular work shift. When school was in session in September 1956, I picked a regular schedule and I drove a trackless trolley, which required special training. I bid on the evening schedule to drive the bus and trolley. That is how I went to Cortez Peters full-time. Being a veteran also helped me with financing my education. The GI Bill allotted thirty-six months to attend college. But I spent seventeen to eighteen months, or half of my GI Bill funds, at Cortez Peters. The other half went to the Baltimore College of Commerce. I went full-time at the Baltimore College of Commerce for two to three months while working, but I could not make it the whole semester while working for the transit company full-time. I would have to finish my college degree on a part-time basis.

The air force placed the desire for education deeply within me. I wanted to go to school like I never had before. I bid on contracts for schedules that would enable me to go to school during the day. Each holiday I also had to bid on a contract or schedule. As I got more seniority, I could almost be guaranteed to get better schedules. After a few years, I got any kind of schedule I wanted.

A terrible thing happened my first year at Cortez Peters while I was driving the bus. I had an accident. A car ran head-on into the bus I was driving, and three people were killed. The driver of the car was the only one who lived. I went home, and they had to put me on medicine because I was so shaken up by what had happened. I was not going to try to drive again. The one passenger that was on my bus in the back also had some injuries. The results of the accident were so bad that the front door on the bus could not open. The police took me to the hospital. Then I had to go to the transit company and make out an accident report. It was so traumatic that I was finished with driving professionally, or so I thought. I had to work the same route and had to cross that bridge every night. And every time

I crossed it, it was painful. The transit company worked with me and brought me back, and I drove seven to eight years more, something I had never thought possible. My relationship with the transit company changed during that incident: I had done well by them, and they had done well by me. There was mutual respect, and I would never forget that they stood beside me during that dark and difficult time.

I majored in business administration and management at Baltimore College of Commerce. At Cortez Peters Business Academy, some people got jobs based on teachers' recommendations from Cortez Peters. But I wanted to get a college degree. I had plans for my future, to either be in business as a CPA or go to law school. Baltimore College of Commerce specialized in people getting CPA or law degrees. But God had other plans for me, and his plans guided me toward choosing social work as my profession.

I was in sociology class. The regular teacher could not be there that day, so we had a substitute teacher. What transpired during that class changed my career and life forever. The substitute treated it almost like a recruitment situation instead of a college lecture. He talked about opportunities in social work, and how social work would help people in communities. He spent ten to fifteen minutes talking about social work and what it would mean to the individual, the community, the country, and to corporations. By the end of the "lecture," I knew that social work sounded like something I wanted to do.

I finished school and took the state test to be a social worker. I scored an eight-five-plus. I received five additional points for being a veteran, putting me in the ninetieth percentile. I took the administrative test and passed.

Why social work? My younger brother and my oldest sister Nina's kids were always in and out of trouble. I saw the social problems in my family, and I thought I could make a lot of difference beyond those domestic walls and in the world. While I was still working at the transit company, the Maryland Training School for Boys called me for an interview. I listed the Baltimore

Transit Company Manager, a White man, as a reference. When I went to his office to resign, he explained how proud he was of me and that he wished other drivers would do the same as I did. I just looked at the community where I was and burned with a desire to want to save the world. Looking back over my life, I figure I have got to be lucky and blessed because everything seemed to turn out for good. Also, looking back over my almost ninety years of experiences, I was both lucky and blessed, and that made all the difference for me and my future successes.

What is your state of being?

1. What are your dreams for your future career-wise?
2. What kind of lifestyle do you want to live?
3. What is preventing you from going for it?
4. What kind of support do you need, and what kind of support do you already have?
5. How long will it take to achieve your dream, and how will you stay motivated?

My hope is that my only child will try and follow in the path that I have carved, God be with her!

CHAPTER 7

The Road to Social Work

There are always those people who make it seem like they are an overnight success and made it to where they are without any struggle, help or challenges along the way. I am not one of them. Never did I feel more acutely the presence of these aspects of life than when I went from college graduate to full-time employee. I am among the first to give credit where credit is due and to acknowledge the difficulties along the way.

The Baltimore College of Commerce tried to get me to go into teaching and education. At that time they had a career path in mind for me that started with teaching, then progressed to being principal or even superintendent. I started in the field of education by substitute teaching. I know what you are thinking: "Weren't you on fire for social work?" Yes, I was, but I explored an alternative before I passed the state job placement exam and started working at the training school in August. Once I knew that I had been accepted at the Maryland Training School for Boys, I would tease my students that were hard to discipline, "If you don't straighten up, you'll join me at the training school." I truly believed that I was in my true vocation and had visions of how the work I was doing would have multiple impacts: on my extended family, at the school, and in society. Some of the kids at the school needed a strong male figure to set them straight.

Occasionally, I would tell them, "You ain't goin' to be nothing if you don't stop acting up and start acting right!" Usually, they would either ignore me or talk back, but one boy responded, "I'm going to be something, Mr. McQueen." I am sorry to say that I just filtered out their responses, positive or negative.

One boy surprised me, however, and found me after a couple of moves and a different and major career change. He called me on the phone several years later. "Mr. McQueen, I'm in the army, married, and have two kids! I told you I was going to be something." Something like that is a once-in-a-lifetime reward that made me feel I truly was making a difference. More commonly, unfortunately, the boys I worked with, either as a volunteer at the community center or as staff at the training school, did not reach their potential or lowered my expectations of them.

A case in point was a community center boy who did not want to stay with his family but stayed with an older woman who had an alcoholic son. I pressed him and pressed him about why he did not want to stay with his own family. Finally, he seemed to yield and stop protesting and agreed to take me to his home. When we got to his home, there was no mother there at that moment. His father was drinking with his buddies, and the boy's siblings, all little children, were just running around. Even worse was that one of the little ones had not been changed in some time. He got me. At that time I was not accustomed to keeping liquor in the house. That night was a turning point; I picked up a bottle before I went home. Jeannette said, "What's going on?" I had a drink and shared my experiences with her.

Shortly after that I got a job at the State of Maryland Headquarters as a research analyst. My entire department consisted of three people: my supervisor, a White girl, and me. The research analyst job paid more than the training school and was at a higher grade in the state employment system. But I did not like that job. I was given work that would only take me two to three days to complete, and I would be expected to make it last for the whole month. I did not get along with the White girl; she did not show it, but I felt it. I told Jeannette I was going to quit the job. She cried and begged me not to. "That's a good job, Bill!" Despite her protesting, I went into my supervisor's office and said, "I don't like this job, and I'm quitting! There is nothing bad about the job. I just don't like it. You understand?"

He did not. But his response was generous and wise. The supervisor listened to me and then taught me a life lesson I would never forget. "Bill," he asked me, "do you have another job?"

I quietly said no.

Then the supervisor said, "You need to keep this job while looking for another job. When you get accepted, tell me. Bill, you should never quit a job without having another job lined up."

One day, while on a coffee break, I saw my former supervisor at the training school, who had been transferred to headquarters. He asked me how I was doing. I told him that I did not like my current job as a research analyst. "How would you like to go back to the training school at the same pay level that you are getting now as a research analyst?" he asked. This was better than anything I could have imagined. He made a call and I had my old job back, with higher pay. To celebrate, Jeannette and I took a New York City vacation, where we saw a show and stayed at a hotel. This trip was not for visiting relatives, like her sister, who lived in the city. This trip was a true vacation, just for fun. We went to clubs and ate dinner out at fine restaurants. Things were looking up!

One day, after I was back at the training school, we were in a meeting. I didn't like what the other teachers and social workers were saying and doing. I banged my fist on the table and roared, "You all are not here for the benefit of the boys! You do not even care about the children! If you don't care about the children, then you shouldn't be in the system!" I stormed out, walking as far away as I could get after my tirade.

My supervisor found me and stated in a calmer way to me than I deserved, "McQueen, I should fire you. But you need help; you need to go to graduate school to learn how to *be* a social worker."

"But I'm doing social work now," I responded, just taking full stock of all that had just happened when I had lost my cool.

"Don't worry, McQueen. I'll keep you on, but you've got to agree you'll get a master's degree in social work. Go to Howard University."

I talked it over with Jeannette. "Okay with me," she said, revealing her support and self-sacrificing nature, which I always knew I could count on.

I applied for graduate school and was accepted at the University of Maryland. I learned that my bachelor's degree from the Baltimore College of Commerce was state accredited but not regionally accredited. This meant that I had to take six hours of credits at a regionally accredited school. So, I attended Coppin State College for three hours and the University of Maryland for three hours. This made it seem like the transition was going to be smooth.

Before I took six credits' worth of courses, however, I went to Howard University to discuss my plans for pursuing a master's in social work. They said they would take me but I would have to do one academic year at Howard because my undergraduate degree came from a state accredited school. It was an easy decision to make. Plus, the University of Maryland was closer to home. Later on I found out that Howard University would not have been the better choice for me. Students were unsatisfied with the social work graduate school and felt it was not teaching them what they needed. They protested and shut it down. Additionally, they could not get jobs in their field. There must have been a guardian angel looking out for me with that situation, sent by the man upstairs as well.

A bachelor's degree was a prerequisite, and I completed the degree that was required. A state civil service exam was required, and I passed that too. I had to make a choice among those jobs for which I was eligible. I thought I could make a difference and help people. I thought I'd make a career of being a civil servant. Time off was a big advantage, and my mother thought I was crazy for giving up this perk of my state job.

After working at the Maryland Training School for Boys for several months, I received a call from the dean of Cortez Peters Business School; he asked me to come and discuss a teaching position at the evening school. I visited the school and talked with the dean and was offered a position teaching three classes three evenings per week. Of course, I accepted the position, which included teaching business mathematics, filing, and world geography.

The business mathematics class was designed to help prepare students to understand and implement business operations, inventory, marketing, sales, and forecasting and find solutions to business problems. The filing class taught the rules of filing and how to set up and manage files. The world geography class helped students to develop skills in making sense of the world around them, such as historical events, whether economic, political, or social. It also helped students to become better thinkers and glean options to pursue in the future.

I worked at Cortez Peters for a little over two years, and I started to attend the University of Maryland School of Social Work. I learned very quickly that working part-time at Cortez Peters and going to the University of Maryland full-time was more than I could handle. So, I stopped teaching and continued pursuing my master's of social work full-time.

Where are you?

1. Do you have a big-picture dream of making a difference?
2. Do you have a personal connection to why you do the work you do?
3. How do you see yourself having an impact on the community/society? Why is this a passion for you?
4. Are you able to qualify for a job that would allow you to contribute in these ways?

When I started to attend the University of Maryland for my master's program, I recorded some bad news. Maryland had frozen scholarships for a year. If I wanted a scholarship, I would have to wait until next year. But I did not want to wait; I decided I wanted to go then. We had no money or salary except what Jeannette and I made. However, we had six apartments we were renting to tenants. Jeannette got a job as a Baltimore teacher, and I had to do her lesson plans. Later on Jeannette worked for Sears as a clerk/typist. We thought that we would be okay with the rental income we had from the six apartments.

For that first year at the University of Maryland, I was without any scholarship and paid my own way. Despite having no extra money for school, we did have a car. It was a new car that was paid for and repeatedly stolen and stripped down. It rapidly became apparent that we did not have enough money to finance this dream on our own. Thankfully, the University of Maryland lent me $1,000, which I had to repay one year after graduation. It was my only option to continue graduate school, so I took it.

I recall that somehow, I talked with a professor/instructor there about my financial problems. Little did I know this casual chat would change my destiny. He asked me, "United Way—ever heard of it?"

I replied, "I think I gave some money to them when I was driving for the transit company."

"Well, they have a scholarship program. You could do your fieldwork in a United Way environment. And when you finish school, not only will you have an MSW and a year of experience, you'll have a job waiting."

Further into the conversation, it became clear that he wanted me to be an executive director of a United Way. He knew all of this because he used to be a regional director for United Way. I filled out the scholarship application papers and sent them in. I got one of the scholarships for year two of my graduate program in social work.

The summer before my second year, I worked at the training school. This was also my first year of summer school for the University of Maryland. The training school gave me half of my time there to do a thesis on the Maryland Training School. I did lots of my research on what I thought would be my thesis topic.

Accepting the United Way (UW) scholarship was not without tough decisions. While the first year I had no money, the second year blessed me with a choice between two scholarships: the UW scholarship and a state scholarship. I was already approved for UW. I was focused on doing clinical work, but decided I could have a greater systemic impact by studying social strategy. I decided not to take the state money but keep the UW scholarship.

Even though encouraged to take and keep both scholarships, I chose the UW one on ethical grounds and stayed away from further researching and writing a thesis on the Maryland Training School for Boys or any other thesis topic because it would have been a lot of work that stopped a lot of people. I decided to take two additional research classes, which enabled me to do a comparative analysis term paper instead. I knew that I was on a good journey; the road to social work was not without its bumps but promised rewarding experience that would lead to a never-dreamed-of twenty-five-year career with UW and the opportunity to leave a professional contribution as a legacy in almost every city where I worked.

I was advised to go to graduate school. The tuition fee was lower. It was convenient to get there either by driving or by bus. I had good professors, mentors, and teachers. This was what I wanted to do with my life. I made this decision to study as a mature adult. I wanted to change the type of social work I was in, and making that change required additional education. I received a scholarship. I received a one-year fieldwork placement working two days a week on a job that was like an internship and prepared me for a full-time job and a twenty-five-year career.

What's your goal?

1. Do you need more education to take the next step in your career?

2. If so, how will you be able to sustain it or afford it?

3. What type of planning, scheduling, or accommodations are necessary to make this possible?

4. Is there anything stopping you from reaching your goals?

5. Do you need to make any personal changes to achieve your next goal or long-term future goal(s)?

6. Have you considered the factors involved in determining where and whether you will go?

*God is pleased when
we care for others.
James 1:26-27 NLT*

*I became a social worker
because I wanted to help
others as many helped me!*

CHAPTER 8

The United Way

Most UWs were either fundraising or counseling organizations. My pre career track / FACTS (Fund and Council Training Scholarship) scholar / graduate school field study mentor thought it would be best if I was in a combined one to start. For example, despite its proximity to home and graduate school, the Baltimore UW was divided into fundraising and counseling. So, in my second and final year of the University of Maryland's MSW program, I did my fieldwork in York, Pennsylvania. The UW there had combined areas in fundraising and counseling, just like my field study mentor (a former UW regional director) had recommended. However, this UW was fifty to sixty miles away from Baltimore, where I lived and attended school at the time. My fieldwork in York took place on Thursdays and Fridays. I tried driving home on Thursday nights and driving back on Friday morning, but it was just too long a commute.

Credit it to the man upstairs or my guardian angels, but the Lord made a way for me to be stay overnight on Thursdays. It was suggested that I go to the Salvation Army to see if they had a place for me. They did and were surprisingly good to me. They offered me the whole floor, with beds, furniture, an equipped kitchen, and a full bathroom in a building that they kept for burn victims and others that were in line with their mission. It was such a good relationship that when I finished my fieldwork with the UW in York, the Salvation Army wanted to hire me. But I declined the offer because it was because of the UW and the FACTS scholar program that I was there in the first place, no matter how good the Salvation Army had been to me.

Over the course of my one year of experience as a FACTS scholar, the York UW treated me like a real professional. True to my mentor's word, while there I got fundraising, allocations, agency relations experience, and even some opportunities to learn about planning for new agencies joining the organization. The purpose of the UW fieldwork experience was to give me exposure to and teach me about the agency and its work. In general, social work fieldwork at the master's level allows you to learn about your specialty area, which was for me social strategy and how social work was in practice. This formative experience with UW was also practical. It led me to my first job and the beginning of a twenty-five-year career with the UW organization.

UW raised money each year for the scholarships. As a FACTS scholar, I was heavily recruited and had my choice of communities in which to work. Two UWs flew me to their locations for an interview, but when it came time to interview with a small UW in Morristown, New Jersey, I elected to drive there from Baltimore. It was the decision of the new executive director to hire me on the spot for this small UW. They needed a third person there. Although my title would be planning and allocations director, I was going to do it all, including fundraising.

At this time UW had few Blacks in the organization and was receiving criticism and pressure about the need to hire more Blacks. My executive director was going to train me for all situations I might encounter as a minority in the organization and in the community. He said he was going to do this because "They treated us Italians the same way." After about two years of complete and comprehensive experience with this small Morris County UW, I had the opportunity to consider going to Princeton, New Jersey, and becoming an executive director for the small one-person UW located there. I passed on the opportunity. It was drilled in me that I needed to stay in whatever job I had with UW for at least three years or be labeled a job-hopper, and I had more to learn in Morristown.

"Can you write grants?" was what some women running daycare centers in the local area asked. I had written grants as a social work graduate student at the University of Maryland and was familiar with how to write them, but by no means was I an experienced grant writer. I asked the UW executive director at Morristown if I could take on this project of writing grants for some daycare centers in the area that needed funding. He said, "No, Bill, you do not have the time." I explained that these ladies did not know how to write grants and could benefit from grant funding. My executive director was firm in his rejection of my spending any of my time on such a project. "Bill, you do not have the time, and you will not do this at UW. You are too busy!"

For him the case was closed, but I liked a professional challenge. So, in the evenings and on the weekends, Jeannette and I wrote a proposal for each of the daycare centers who needed the grant funding, using a standard format we created for each one. One day I received a call from the state about the daycare grant applications. It turned out they liked our grant application model and funded all the daycare centers. A short while later, the state called me back. They needed someone to coordinate all the newly funded daycare centers in Morris County. The state wanted me to write a grant for this position. They came back a third time requesting that I write a grant to fund programs for senior citizens. I wrote a proposal and got a grant for the senior citizen program as well.

Although he had been adamant about my not writing grants as a part of the UW, my executive director in Morristown wanted to take credit for it after it gained success. I went there as the third person; now I had two people, the grant-funded program coordinators, reporting to me. That was almost more than the executive director himself! When I was ready to leave this first UW professional position, the board asked if I wanted to make any comments. I totaled the money I was able to bring into this UW via grants, not just fundraising, and stated that this should be the trend.

I also left my mark on the Morris County UW with the Boys Club, whose director was not performing the way he should have been. I had done a comparative analysis in graduate school and used this as my research tool to do a study all over the country of other Boys Clubs. This led to him losing his job, and he was livid about it, and in his anger, he blamed me. All of that happened in the two and a half years I was at that UW facility.

Just because there was a push to hire more Blacks throughout the UW organization, this did not mean that those who were hired were embraced by the communities that the agencies served when it came to basic needs like housing. We tried on our own to get a decent apartment in a good neighborhood that was safe and well-kept. There was only one way to get a decent apartment back then close to the UW in Morristown or in the nearby community of Morris County: Blacks had to go through a certain organization that found places for our people to live. This surrounding community was the headquarters for international organizations such as Allied Chemical and Warner Lambert, and it was just outside of New York.

The organization that helped us find an apartment had to get a White woman to pose like she was getting the apartment. We ended up getting an apartment in Dover, New Jersey, and once we were moved in there, everything was fine and we were accepted, but getting the place without the help of that organization's bait and switch would have been impossible. Here I was bringing in all kinds of money to the Morris County UW and getting funding for programs at the state level, and I could not even find a decent place to live for my family. This was a hiccup, but overall the Morris County UW launched my career and set a foundation for me that others at the national level followed very seriously.

UW of America in Alexandria, Virginia, was my next professional move. It was at UW of America that I found out that the FACTS scholarship program had been discontinued and replaced with the internship program I started. I knew that without the FACTS scholarship, I probably would not have been able to finish the University of Maryland's MSW program.

My mentor at the University of Maryland had literally contacted the person in charge of the scholarship and helped me get it. It also marked a turning point in my transition from graduate student to career social worker in social strategy and community organization.

Once I was in the headquarters of UW, they wanted me to close out the scholarship program so I could develop an internship program, which initially made me sad. However, for the individuals that served as interns with UW, it allowed a broader selection pool than just MSWs. The internship would allow interns to get experience in fundraising, planning and allocations, and agency relations. My job at UW of America was working in human resources. I put people on a career development track: I asked them what their goals in UW were, collaborated with them to determine what should be their next move/ job, and clearly established what they wanted to get out of UW by making sure that they were accepting of the fact that in a career at UW, rising on the career ladder meant that they were going to be moving. Ironically, my experiences as a FACTS scholar and the mentoring I had gotten in graduate school, as well as my first UW job in New Jersey, helped me to become a better mentor for other UW employees. It also enabled me to do my part in hiring more Blacks as UW professionals.

To reach both the goals of the internship and diverse recruiting, I had to recruit at different types of universities. I did not just go to elite institutions. I had to find people from all walks of life. Not just Harvard and not just MSWs, but a mixture of people. I went to HBCUs like Howard University and Atlanta University. I started with a packet, and a recent college graduate helped me by condensing the information from a packet with "too much info" to a one-page folded pamphlet.

Then came my recruiting trip to Wharton. The president of the UW of America had to be in New York for a meeting. Never had anyone told me what I should present. I thought that this would be the end of my career with UW. I was informed that we would travel together, and

I should make him an outline on what he should talk about. "Tell him what to say." My outline was broad. It covered fundraising, planning and allocations, agency relations, and a willingness to move around if you wanted to move up. My secretary typed it, and the president looked at it and just said, "Okay" but nothing to indicate if he thought the outline was good or bad. At the end of our day at Wharton, he said, "Stay here until you interview all of them." He went on to his meeting in New York, and I stayed behind and followed his orders. After I was back at headquarters, my immediate supervisor said, "The president was impressed." Once I developed my guide, the local UWs in a lot of communities where we did not go nonetheless interviewed using the guide because it had the approval of the president of UW of America.

For the internship program, I remember I had an interview with an intern I sent to Atlanta. He was not doing well, and the vice president of UW sent me to Atlanta to check on him and help him get better adjusted. This intern was from Chicago and not used to a lot of Whites. I would work with the intern after he got off work but took tour buses and got a lot of experience with the city of Atlanta. I kept my eyes open. The new associate executive director in Atlanta was looking to hire staff a few months after he moved there. I got a good feel for Atlanta. I also learned to tell people about my weaknesses and let them decide if I was a good fit or not. I learned this from an interview at a UW in Columbia. The associate executive director said, "Whatever you write, I'll look at it, and we'll make changes to it." After a few months, he said I did not need his help any longer. I gave a writing test to the people I hired. I did not want somebody on my staff whose English had to be corrected. I took a chance and shared my most vulnerable weak spot and let others support me in it, and it worked out.

At the UW of Metropolitan Atlanta, I interviewed for a research position. They interviewed me but thought I sounded more like an agency relations director. They made a place for me, and we moved to Atlanta. One of the staff members who was supposed to be showing me around and letting me tour and take in the sites of Atlanta foreshadowed a very challenging moment once I was on staff: a radio interview justifying why I had been chosen by UW of America for the job when there were qualified people in the metropolitan Atlanta area. In the radio interview, they asked me why I had gotten the job, why I had been brought there, and other grueling, stressful questions on the air in a thirty to forty-five minute solo interview. I survived it.

Jeannette and I were looking for a house. We were working with a Black female realtor. Then we found a house that we both fell in love with. The current homeowner was a retired realtor and retired military person. There were not a lot of black people living in the neighborhood we settled on. We did not buy the house with the swimming pool because we had a young daughter who did not know how to swim, but we fell in love with a house fronting the lake. We decided we would buy it. We attended the Christmas party for UW professional staff. There was a White woman realtor at the party who asked us where the house we had decided on was located. After we told her, she replied, "Why, Blacks do not live in East Point nor on Carriage Way! You are going to have problems." Merry Christmas.

I do not know how or why it happened, but the real estate paper processor called me directly while I was at work at UW. He said, "Mr. McQueen, you can buy this house without any down payment as a veteran." At the time there were only two other Black families living in the community. In less than a year, most of the people living there were Black. That is the South as it was and unfortunately still is.

UW of Atlanta had bad agency relations, and it wanted the agency evaluations that Rochester, New York, was receiving. This was one of the jobs assigned to me. Every agency was not evaluated at the same time, and the process required meetings and explanations, and it took a year to go through the entire process. After a year UW would watch and see if they adhered correctly to the allocations process.

I came in at the end of January to work with UW of Atlanta. In October I became agency relations and allocations director. The previous allocations director had left to be a professor at Atlanta University full-time. He was doing both jobs, UW and AU. The next January they increased my duties and gave me a raise. I became the planning, allocations, and agency relations director. My immediate supervisor at UW of America had told me this would happen; he predicted that if I worked hard, I would get a pay increase, so I should not worry about leaving the UW of America for UW of Atlanta at the same pay. But there was one problem: I was working constantly, starting at 4:00 a.m. most mornings and before going to church on Sundays. I confided in the guy who had taken me on the tour of the sights of Atlanta and foreshadowed the interview. I told him I was working too hard. I even turned relaxing and spirituality into a competition by taking on stewardship at my church and fundraising for them.

A good family doctor put me on tranquilizers; he told me I was doing too much. He ordered me to stay off work for a week or a couple of weeks. He wanted me to get out in the yard and enjoy gardening for health planting. He also started me walking for stress relief. I returned to UW and told my associate executive director / supervisor about it. He responded, "Bill, you don't know how to delegate! I am going to give you some tapes to get the monkeys off your back. Do not play them at home or at the job. This is strictly a car training program." Later, at a going away party for the associate executive director, I dumped the tapes on his head.

I got sick from not knowing how to work with people. A week or two weeks off, and then he was able to get the meds set. I also got sick at my cousin's house with bleeding ulcers and had to be hospitalized for a week. This was at the time we were going to leave Atlanta. I was weaker than I should have been, but no one seemed to notice or say anything. This marked my second time in the hospital for ulcers; the first time was at Baltimore College of Commerce as a student.

Another lesson I learned about my professional requirements and personal definition of success was that it was important for people to know me. Therefore I went to human resources at UW of America. The new president of UW of Atlanta wanted me to stay in Atlanta. I also learned that they loved me in Atlanta because I oversaw allocations and money. This was true once I got to Memphis and oversaw agency relations and training development. This became superevident when a guy at a cocktail party just walked away after he found out that I was not in charge of money and could not help his wife's agency get more from United Way.

At the UW of Greater Memphis, my chief success was the creation of a Youth United Way. It had a Youth UW board and structure so that the youth could distribute money any way they wanted, and the Youth UW extended from day-care through college fundraising. They kept their money separate. The Youth UW board decided where they wanted it to go. It was called "A Dime's Worth of Difference," and it started in preschool and went through college. My goal was to teach youth how to contribute to make places better for people. That model was replicated by UW all over America. We even took youth to the UW conferences. I was especially proud of a young Black twelfth grade girl from Memphis who was selected to be the Youth UW speaker in Washington, DC, with UW people all over the country and Vice President Bush there too. She demonstrated giving the biggest contribution by serving as leader of the Youth UW.

UW of Cincinnati, Ohio, put the brakes on me. They did not want me and were about to fire me. My executive director was on vacation, out of the country. They would not let me do what he had hired me to do, like develop a Youth UW. The women working for me wanted to get rid of me. Among the people I worked with, I did not have support; this was true even from the board that hired me. If we tried to do what we wanted to do, they would fire my executive director, who was responsible for bringing me to the agency. This was the only time I ever saw a psychiatrist. Jeannette advised me that I had a good job and I should just mark my time until I retired. Oddly enough, the psychiatrist said the same thing. "If your boss is happy and he'll go along with it, keep the job until you retire." Cincinnati was the only place I did not feel that I left my mark. I had planned to retire at sixty-two. Jeannette passed when I was sixty-one, and I applied for my social security in January to fulfill my plan, the first time I made a significant decision alone.

Some of the board members thought my executive director was trying to force me out. I reached an agreement that extended my work at the agency over a year and got so busy that I forgot I had earlier applied for social security. My account grew, and I had to write social security and had to pay them back. As I neared my new retirement age, I had to come up with a plan for my retirement that I would enjoy as a widower.

I owed UW a minimum of one year of service as a result of the scholarship they had given me. This was the field of social work I had gone to school for, and I felt like I was really prepared to do that kind of work after the one-year fieldwork experience I had acquired while at UW. One of the things I liked about UW was the ability to move from one agency to another. I enjoyed moving around to different communities, and I made my mark in every community except one. My family was supportive of the moves.

Why not you?

1. Have you determined what you want to do with your life?
2. Have you looked at what it would take to accomplish those dreams / that vision?
3. Who will you need to rely on to get you there?
4. How will you remove obstacles in the way of getting you there?
5. What significant relationships can you forge in the place where you work/live?
6. What is required to make you feel good/ great about what you are doing?

God has been a constant leader and protector even during those times when I could not feel His presence!

CHAPTER 9

The Union Institute

Around the time of my retirement, I was trying to decide how I would spend my newly increased free time. I wanted something that would challenge me, so I was deciding between going to law school or getting my PhD. I still had a lot of energy, and I remembered how my Daddy, Dock McQueen, had advised against sitting around doing nothing. I needed more information. Chase Law School, across the Ohio river in Northern Kentucky, offered the opportunity for prospective students to visit the campus and sit in on classes. When I sat in on my first law school class, I instantly noticed the role of technology in the classroom among the law students. *Those folks are serious over there!* I thought. Based on that visit, I determined once and for all that law school was just not for me after years and years of wanting to become a lawyer and dreaming about how my life would have been different had I been able to go to law school.

One of my coworkers at the United Way of Cincinnati was always trying to get me to get my PhD. He had gone to the Union Institute and was a heavily involved social worker. Little by little he encouraged me to get my PhD. Slowly I considered it, and as I have mentioned, by the time I was at the age of sixty-three, I was retired. I started my PhD studies with the Union Institute. I was never disappointed with my choice of studies. For a retired person, the Union Institute was a good match for me at that stage of life, both age-wise and professionally.

I wanted to get a PhD in business administration, but "those in the know" counseled me to just do whatever was the easiest area in which to get the "doctor" title, which was 90 percent of why I was pursuing graduate school at this stage in my life. When it came down to it, I really wanted to do volunteer work with youth. So, I was advised that a public administration degree would be a better fit given my goals and experience. I signed up and was on my way to becoming Dr. McQueen. The Union Institute let you go as fast or as slow as you wanted to go. It was kind of like a Montessori School for adults.

I always thought adults did not try enough to help youth by speaking words of success, encouragement, and positivity to them, the future generation, something as simple as "You're going to be special someday" or "You can do it if you want and set your mind to it" (words spoken by my mama and daddy, respectively). Mentors while I was young and at crucial decision-making crossroads had made such a difference in my life. As a social worker and later at United Way, I always believed "you touch a few people and make a huge difference in their life." But deciding to work with youth was more like focusing on group work rather than the social strategy in which I specialized.

Working at the Maryland Training School, I quickly discovered that many of the youth that wound up in the training school did not have mentors, parents, grandparents, or guardians that told them that on a consistent basis nor those who spoke success into them like my parents had for me. It was rare and greatly appreciated when a child or adolescent would come back and demonstrate that they had beat the odds. This was true with a young man I challenged to become something and somebody while he was at the Maryland Training School, as I discussed above. Years later he found me, tracking me down after my many different jobs and moves. He had joined the army as a career and had a wife and two children. It was important to him that I knew that he had become something and somebody just because of my challenge to him at the Maryland Training School to do so.

I spent about two and half years at the Union Institute earning my PhD. When I started my classes, I did work, but I was not working long. I followed my counselor's advice and decided what my major would be: public administration. This counselor had a PhD, and he was also a close friend. He joined my doctoral committee and recruited a colleague of his from Cleveland to join the committee. Learners at the Union Institute had to have a committee, and the chairman of the committee had to be on staff at the institute. The second co-reader I chose was someone I had known throughout my United Way career. All my writing went to him. He would look at my diverse and numerous written reports in a critical way. There was also a young thirtysomething guy trying to get a PhD that I selected. I figured that through his working at the Union Institute he would be able to go to school for free. Something happened, and he did not finish. All total I ended up with six people on my committee. With people that were not local, I would also arrange for them to fly in for conferences and other meetings that could not be done by phone.

The Union Institute had people from all over the world. I took thirteen courses there. The Institute also allowed me to create my own courses. Other students could attend. You could have an outside instructor to teach it, or you could teach it yourself. These courses were as short as one day or a three-day seminar. The Union Institute left it all up to you. Scholars had to write their own reports. After completing the written work for the courses, scholars had to send it to their chair and their committee for them to review it and to approve it. My counselor and good friend helped me to develop a standard format for the reports I had to write. This helped while I worked to plan a conference. After I planned it, I had to advertise it so people would come. True to its expectations of self-directed scholars, the Union Institute had us create the standard we used for ourselves. A good point for me about my doctoral program was that scholars did not have to have a lot of credits, just sixty-six for their national doctoral program. The Union Institute managed the conference number and other scholars created conferences because there were a certain number of conferences you had to attend.

There were so many courses/conferences that sometimes there were three to four people attending the course and sometimes there were up to fifteen or twenty of us. Sometimes courses would meet at the library or at a person's home; they allowed you to set it up how and where you wanted. The classes took time, as did meeting with my committee. Just because this unique program was self-directed and self-organized did not mean that there were no rules in setting up the different aspects of one's doctoral program. After making sure there was a certain number of people from the Union Institute staff, the school had a model you followed. You paid them an amount each month to be enrolled, and that was based on how many credits you wanted to complete that quarter. Each time you took a course, you had to describe it in writing to make sure it would meet the standards of the institution.

I determined that my dissertation had to be on strategic planning. Here was my rationale. Lots of agencies would do a strategic plan in UW. The concern was that they never did anything that was based on that strategic plan. My dissertation zeroed in on agencies to see if they followed up on strategic plans in practice. I developed surveys. I just picked out certain new agencies and compared them. The title of my dissertation was "An Identification of Strategic Planning Components and Processes Among Newly Formed Nonprofit Organizations in the Greater Cincinnati Area."

For me, this doctoral experience was fantastic. These professionals trusted me, thus enhancing and further developing my learning style. It was learning for learning's sake and was for the first time able to just read and learn what I wanted to know about a subject in a deeper way. I wanted something to do, and my doctoral studies gave me that. I also wanted to make a strong contribution to scholarship in my area of study using the twenty-five-years of career insights I had gleaned while working with UW. I felt this was a tangible way of leaving my mark on the Cincinnati UW. After completing my dissertation and earning my degree, I moved to Atlanta within six months.

It was a cap off to my career to get a doctorate. In retirement, it was important to stay busy and challenged. Doing something to make a difference was still important to me. The doctorate also opened a few more doors professionally, socially, financially, and in terms of volunteer opportunities. Also, I did not feel it was too late to learn at age sixty-three. I sought to compare real-world experience with intellectual/academic theory.

Why not you?

1. Is there something you want to do or learn that you never wanted to before?

2. Is there an area in which you can make a difference or significant contribution?

3. Is there something you are / have always been curious about?

4. Do you want people to consider you differently from what/who you are now based on all or some of your life's experiences?

5. Is there something you want to know or show that will change the way the world works or allow the world to see things differently because of your influence?

6. What kinds of outcomes/measures will make such a change worthwhile for you?

I have tried to care for others and not only about myself.
Jude 1:12-13 NLT

I pray that I did not miss the mark!

CHAPTER 10

Ellen, My Georgia Peach

Let me say we knew a lot of people in common before we knew each other. We spent a lot of time on the phone talking with each other before we met face-to-face. Even after we got serious, we seldom saw each other in person before we explored whether we should marry. We can also be proud that we made it through a special "retreat" where we talked, discussed, and interacted over a weekend, speaking about our future goals and desires, how we handle money, and what expenses we have—the kinds of things that most couples do not do prior to marrying. After marrying, we hosted six black-tie, red carpet, by-invitation-only Christmas parties, celebrated fifteen years of being partners in business, and had a surprise "twenty-five year" anniversary celebration. I ultimately proclaim and loudly cheer that I am still hangin' in and hangin' on, for better or for worse, with my "Georgia Peach," Ellen Robinson Wade-McQueen.

I was introduced to Ellen, my second wife, by a close platonic female friend who knew both of us. It was her brother-in-law who vetted me for her; since I knew him the entire eight years that I was in Atlanta working as a vice president at United Way, he helped me get adjusted to the city. We had been more than just colleagues. For example, I remember when he came to my office and told me his brother (Ellen's late husband) was sick and in the hospital. I remember when he told me that his brother had passed away. I also learned over the course of that long, activity-filled weekend that Ellen once served on a UW allocations panel with 250 people and did so with a guy from Coca-Cola. It is possible that

I met her during that experience. Additionally, I also knew her "brother" Bob Jennings because we were both in Leadership Atlanta around the same time. So there had been several chances for Ellen and I to meet, yet we never did. We both had something sorrowful in common, as well, because both of us had lost a spouse.

I will always remember visiting Atlanta for our first date after talking on the phone with her for hours before we met. It seemed that Ellen and her friends had something special and entertaining planned from the moment I got off the plane until the moment I returned to Cincinnati. I should have expected something different from what I was used to when this full weekend started with a delayed Cincinnati–Atlanta flight. I started off tired from traveling and with low energy for our first in-person meeting.

Ellen, along with our mutual friend who had introduced us and a male friend of hers, picked me up from the airport. From there it was nonstop. We went directly to Chastain Park for a concert, then went jazz clubbing following the concert and then to Ellen's house, where our mutual friend stayed overnight because Ellen was insistent on not staying alone, even in her own home, with me since we had just met. The three of us slept in separate bedrooms. Saturday night was a bit better because I was more rested, but it was still fast-paced. We went to her brother-in-law's high school reunion and to a club, where I danced with Ellen for the first time. My goal that weekend was to spend some time with her, getting to know her better. When I got ready to leave for Cincinnati, she and the female friend took me to the airport. I was so tired I was glad to get out of the car. But all in all, it was a great weekend. I kept saying to myself, *Ellen is one senior citizen full of energy.*

What I discerned during the weekend visit was that she seemed stable, living by herself, and was about something. In addition to several Atlanta contacts we had in common, we also had ballroom dancing, and I was learning how to dance as a way to have a hobby that would keep my mind off the recent loss of my first wife.

I remember that one weekend the NAACP was hosting a conference in Nashville, Tennessee. I wanted to go so I could see Ellen who would be in attendance, but my executive director was going to have a staff meeting for the managers at his house on the same Saturday, which was rare. I requested permission to skip the meeting, and he allowed me to do so. We had dinner together that Saturday evening, and that night we spent time together away from the conference. While I was with UW of Memphis, I served on the NAACP Board of Directors. I had never been to a national conference and looked forward to the chance to see some friends and colleagues from Memphis who were involved in the organization. This was the second time I saw Ellen and again was reassured that she was someone I wanted to get to know better.

Both of us liked making an impact and leaving our mark wherever we went. One time, after we started visiting each other in our respective cities, Ellen toyed with the idea of our hosting a Christmas party. Not an average, run-of-the-mill party, but one that would be held two days after Christmas and would be different from anything Atlanta had experienced in a while, if ever. Of course we decided it would be black-tie, tuxedos for the men and evening gowns for the ladies. There would also be red carpet and parking attendants.

We made sure to invite those individuals who had extended invitations to us during the year. I remember one woman who had not been invited showing up anyway. It was the affair of the year, and everybody wanted to be on the invite list. The idea, style, and scale of the party were legendary, unparalleled, and different. Our guest list also included persons we wanted to get to know. A hundred people were invited. Often we had special entertainment such as Nat King Cole's brother, who played our baby grand piano, and other colleagues of Ellen's who performed.

Things progressed with our long-distance Atlanta–Cincinnati relationship. Sometimes Ellen flew to me, and other times I flew down to Atlanta to be with her, especially since her daughter, who worked for the airlines, could get us a buddy pass. When I did not fly, I drove just to be with her.

After a short while, we discussed taking our relationship to the next level. This is when I suggested the retreat so that we could discuss and explore issues that many couples never discuss prior to becoming serious, especially issues that would impact a marriage.

The retreat was held in Knoxville, Tennessee, which is halfway between our two cities. Ellen got lost and could not find the hotel. She ended up in another hotel, and I had to go and get her. When she got ready to return to Atlanta, she asked me to take her back to the first hotel so she could easily find her way out of the city.

Our story of marrying after twenty-five years deserved to be celebrated, and we were able to do so with family and friends, more than fifty of them. I decided to throw a surprise twenty-fifth anniversary party. I asked her daughter, Rhonda, to take charge. Rhonda wanted to have the party at a hotel, but I wanted it to be at our home, since we had a ballroom that would accommodate up to 150 people. Just as it seemed as though we were running out of options, we thought about having it at one of Ellen's closest girlfriend's homes. Her girlfriend graciously agreed that we could use her very spacious home.

I invited and flew my brothers (Bobby and Frankie) from Baltimore for the party. Despite my best efforts to keep it from Ellen, I believe someone told her what was planned. When it came to the day and time of the actual celebration, Ellen kept finding excuses not to go. Finally, all four of us, Ellen, two brothers and me, got in the car and drove to the party.

At the time we met, as is true now, there were several qualities that made Ellen the ideal mate for me. Included in these qualities are 1) she is a social networker; 2) she has a head for business; 3) she is a strategic thinker; 4) we have common goals, principles, and beliefs; 5) we have the common background of losing a spouse to death; and 6) we are both hard workers. All of these are qualities I believe will keep a couple together.

I can recall that during that first phone conversation, even before we met physically, she asked some good questions that caused me to do some deep thinking. She helped me develop a process of thinking about what I wanted to do with my life beyond retirement. She was instrumental in developing and implementing plans on how I could use my skills, talents, interests, and expertise to fit different social, economic, and environmental situations. She appeared to fit in well with my environment and my family members and colleagues. She expressed big dreams of what she wanted to do and become. She encouraged me to pursue and complete the PhD. She motivated me to join Alpha Phi Alpha fraternity, and she motivated me to go into the childcare business.

When we first met, I had sold my home and moved into an apartment. She influenced my decision to move back to Atlanta after retiring from United Way.

She was also instrumental in selling our childcare businesses and helped me to transition successfully into full retirement. She suggested taking up the hobby of playing bridge and joined me in ballroom dancing, something that I love to do. She skillfully plans and manages our home budget, and has upgraded my wardrobe to include different colors and kinds of clothing. She is the yin to my yang!

Why not you?

1. What are you concerned about regarding a second marriage? What are you excited about regarding the relationship? What scares you about taking this step?

2. Would you be willing to use a rubric from your faith community or the help of a professional relationship counselor before entering into another marriage?

3. What do you bring to the marital relationship?

4. What is your plan for the future together?

5. Are you willing to compromise and be the first to apologize for the sake of the union?

6. Are you a full and complete individual apart from the marriage?

7. What kind of support will you offer and need to keep the marriage strong and ongoing?

Love helps people in their difficulty.
Philippians 4:11-14 NLT

Not that I was ever in need, for I have learned how to be content with whatever I have. I know how to live on almost nothing or with everything. For I can do everything through Christ, who gives me strength.

CHAPTER 11

My Move Back to Atlanta

After retiring from UW, I spent the years 1994 to 1996 working on my doctoral degree and closing out things in Cincinnati. Even though I never figured myself much of a dancer, I did a lot of ballroom dancing at a private dance school. For any reason I tried to use why I should not take ballroom dancing lessons, the instructors had a reason why I should. According to them, if you can walk, you can dance. "Can you walk? Were you in the air force? Then you can dance. Miss a step? Why just step back in! Look at it all in terms of exercise and fun." The first time we went out dancing, Ellen danced with my instructor. Ellen had been dancing all her life, so she moved with ease, and it seemed easy for her to pick up steps. After all of these years of angrily sitting on the outside of the dance floor and looking at others enjoying themselves, moving in time to the music, and having fun, I believed that these lessons would be my ticket to join them and be a part of the heart of the party.

When Ellen and I would dance together, people would just sit down and watch us. I used to be afraid of people watching me dance, but now, after lessons, I welcomed it and even liked to show off my skills a little. That made the dance lessons all worthwhile. My first wife, Jeannette, used to beg me to dance. I thought people would look at me and laugh. She tried to teach me that it was all about having fun. In some way, her passing was my motivating force. Back then and throughout our married life, I would get mad with Jeannette and take her home if she even asked me to join her on the dance floor. With Ellen, once we added an entertainment room to our ranch-style home with everything on one floor (our "ballroom," we called it), we held dance parties with on-site private group lessons for anyone who wanted to increase their confidence by learning the steps for a few of the dances we knew.

Things moved right along, and Ellen and I married in 1994 at my church, Allen Temple AME church in Cincinnati, right after I retired. Despite our change in status from single to married, Ellen stayed in Atlanta and I stayed in Cincinnati. We decided to keep our marriage secret for two-plus years, the time it would take me to finish my doctoral degree and set things up so that I could move to Atlanta. Although we did not get married in the Catholic Church until I moved to Atlanta, two-plus years later, we felt that our marriage, although it had taken place in my Christian (but Protestant) church, would not be acceptable until and unless our marriage took place in the Catholic Church where Ellen was a member. So, we held a small family gathering and marriage ceremony in the Catholic Church.

While in Cincinnati, I entertained myself by doing ballroom dancing and attending dances. It is clearer to me now: I was alone in Cincinnati while my first wife stayed in Memphis so our daughter could graduate high school, and it was the end of my first wife's life; I was alone while my daughter finished her last year of college at Princeton University; and I was alone most of the time while my second wife Ellen was in Atlanta and I was in Cincinnati while we dated and at the start of our married life.

Visiting back and forth from Cincinnati to Atlanta, the driving got to be long and exhausting those first two years. For me, it was a comfortable ride in my new cherry red Cadillac, a gift to myself once I retired. One time I was driving in the Cadillac through Tennessee on my way to see Ellen, and a state trooper pulled me over for speeding. Although the trooper complimented me on my pretty retirement gift, he said that I should use the cruise control feature that the car was equipped with so I would not break the speed limit. And then he wrote me a ticket, which he gave me with a smile. I was glad Ellen's daughter worked for the airlines, enabling her to fly for free, so travel was less of a time commitment for her.

I never let on, but I was on the fence about moving to Atlanta. After retirement it looked like I might have a follow-up career in the insurance industry. The opportunity was in Cincinnati, not Atlanta. I knew that Ellen would have a hard time cutting ties in Atlanta to relocate permanently to Cincinnati. She played it cool, yet it was evident to me that she liked the idea of having a business too. I think all the insurance company wanted were my one hundred or so contacts and not to have me as a salesman. They wrote me a rejection letter about not being the right fit since I did not have to work because I had retirement income coming in. This nest egg was a drawback in their minds. For them, I was not sufficiently "hungry" because I did not need to work.

I still find it amazing that I started off in Aynor, South Carolina, and ended up in Atlanta, Georgia. Although there had been some changes, like churches and neighborhoods, it remained the place where I had stayed longer than any other when I was working with United Way and where I fit in better than any other place. Now, with a new wife, it became home once again!

Once I embraced retirement, I had plans to enjoy myself and volunteer in Atlanta. I would reconnect with people, engage in regular new friend meetings, such as getting to know Ellen's friends and accompanying her to parties, join and get involved with the 100 Black Men of Atlanta, and expand my network and keep active in the Alpha Phi Alpha fraternity that Ellen had suggested I join as a way to fit in better with numerous social groups. After all, Ellen belonged to a lot of social groups. It was ballroom dancing that must have saved her after she became a widow. About a year after I had moved back to Atlanta and plugged in to my new actively social retirement lifestyle, our lives were about to change significantly and for the long term. A mentor of Ellen's put a bug in her ear about going into the childcare business.

Coming home from church one Sunday, we talked casually about seeing if we could find a place for sale that could be the location for our idea-only childcare business, and lo and behold, we turned onto Creel Road and saw a For Sale sign in the yard of a house that looked like it just might do. As it turned out, they had just put the sign up that morning. We told them we would buy the house. The wife and co-owner of the Creel Road property said she had to talk with her husband about it. We asked her to communicate to him that we wanted them to take the sign down. At that point I had no idea what I was getting into, but slowly and surely, I was about to find out firsthand the ins and outs of bringing a new small business to a residential neighborhood.

Remember, I had a barbershop and rented apartments in multifamily houses, both at a young age, and had a background in business with my college degree. The barbershop helped put coins in my mama's pocket while I was in the air force, and the apartments helped with steady income while I was at the University of Maryland for graduate school, working on my master's in social work.

I expected nothing less than success with the daycare business based on my previous business experiences as a successful owner and operator.

It was my belief then, as it is now, that there is no limit to one's potential. I was determined to push this principle to its furthest point as a late-blooming entrepreneur in the fast-paced world of the childcare business.

I fell in love with Atlanta the first time I came to visit. I stayed in Atlanta eight-plus years, longer than for any other United Way assignment. My first wife died, and a friend's introduction to the woman who became my second wife made this move viable since this was her hometown. I became a part of a social network such that it was very enjoyable to be in Atlanta. It is also more economical to live here compared to other major cities.

Why not you?

1. Have you considered a significant move at a time in your life marked by change?
2. Are you satisfied with where you are living?
3. Is there a place you have visited or lived that you would like to return to?
4. Where is your strongest social network located?
5. How would you fit in with a new community?

I have taken comfort
in Jeremiah 29:11

*Knowing that it is not a promise
to immediately rescue us from
hardship or suffering, but
rather a promise that God has
a plan for our lives regardless
of our current situation. This
has been my saving grace!*

CHAPTER 12

GEMS Childcare

I was the quasi grandfather of 4,251 "grandchildren." They called me "Mr. Bill"! Does that sound crazy? It might be, but we lived, worked, ate, slept, and dreamed of childcare. Let me tell you how it happened. Both of us after being retired a while still had a lot of energy left, even with dancing and clubs to fill our time. We thought it might be good to have our own business. So, we checked out owning and running an assisted living home for senior citizens. Somehow this was not quite the right fit. A former colleague of Ellen's who was in the childcare business let

Ellen know she wanted to sell her daycare center. Even though we did not buy hers since she ultimately sold the center to one of her employees, the idea of owning and operating a childcare center stuck. My notion was "I'm not going to be outdone; we'll create our own, and it will be better than any other childcare facility."

We started "small," with about fifty-three children. We quickly learned that at a real small center, you work hard but you do not yield much profit. Once we got into the business, we found out that one should never have a childcare center smaller than one hundred children. It was just not worth the trouble. Dock McQueen, my late father, was right when he said, "Education is expensive…it costs a lot; but once you get it, you've learned from it." Based on his wisdom in that statement, with childcare, we were about to learn billions of dollars in lessons about the business.

Zoning was a big challenge even after we acquired the house where we wanted to set up our childcare center. The house was in a mostly residential neighborhood with a school nearby. We would have our hands full for the next few years before we opened. Starting out we also knew we would need to do some massive renovations to meet the needs of the children and qualify for a license. The neighbors' reaction to bringing a childcare center into the neighborhood was mixed. Some of the neighborhood people were cooperative, and some were not. Overall, however, the neighborhood was more cooperative than we thought they would be. We were invited to meet with the community association president and then to attend a regular meeting to see if they would be more amenable to us bringing our business to the area. We had to be zoned before bringing an architect in to start the renovation process; we had to make sure we could put our business in there first. The community association presentation was mild compared to the zoning board presentation we had to make.

After what seemed like massive hoops to jump through and a long time paying the note on an empty house, we were approved. But we were just getting started.

We had to address the plumbing system, which had a septic tank. If you have never had experience with a septic tank before, here is how it works: A septic tank functions according to how many people are living there. We knew we would need a bigger one with the influx of people we expected for our business. The sewage line was way down the street. In order to get a permit, they required us to go on a sewage line. We would have to tie into the sewage line and bring it down. Ultimately, they gave us a permit only because a commissioner told them that we knew and to give it to us.

Traffic was also a major consideration. We needed one way in and one way out. Additionally, the closest fireplug needed to be moved a short distance before we could work on the parking lot for the daycare center. The Creel Road property was in the city of College Park, but we had to pay the City of Atlanta to move it. Days, weeks, and months passed, and they never moved it despite our begging and pleading. Once again, we needed help. A friend of Ellen's helped. The husband of her friend called and got it done from Washington, DC. We spent four months waiting until he called and told us it was done.

As if it had not been "fun" enough the first time, we had to go through zoning twice. The engineer who had drawn up the plans for the renovation had left out one part of the carport. We wanted to make the after school room a little bigger. But our hands were tied before we could do so, due to needing that section of the property to be zoned first.

Finally, we were zoned and ready to undertake the renovations. We had used my retirement fund for the deposit. The expense that you must not forget is the note on the property. From 1997 to 2001, we paid the note from my retirement funds. All of this "education" added up. We went to a bank in Atlanta and then to a Black bank I had transferred my retirement to and used to pay the down payment for our first childcare center. Both banks turned us down. Our next effort was with a bank in Fayetteville, where we wanted to borrow $125,000 to renovate the facility, in addition to the mortgage loan we had already taken out. It was a challenge, but we went through all of that. We did manage to get some good out of this situation. Ellen's stepson lived in the house before the renovations started, and he had the whole place to himself and was not charged rent, but we did not have to worry about someone breaking in, which happens when houses sit empty.

Once funded, renovations got started and our education continued. We had to close the whole kitchen in since we were using the building as a childcare center. We did not know about that requirement; thus, education does cost.

We called our childcare business "GEMS" and came up with the motto "Where every child sparkles." Our license for GEMS 1 (a.k.a. Gems Learning Academy) was for fifty-three children. This was good for us because we did not know the childcare business. As I have mentioned, we found out that we would need at least one hundred children to make the kind of profit we desired. We ran GEMS 1 from February 2001 to

2011, but in 2005 we learned about possibility of starting and running a GEMS 2, and in the spring of 2006, we broke ground for a multimillion-dollar facility.

Before that happened, God had more "lessons" for us to learn. Some of the things we learned about at GEMS 1 would benefit us at the second GEMS. These lessons included the food service program, dealing with staff, and the ins and outs of the management of a larger childcare center. One of the hardest aspects of the business was making sure there was always a responsible person in charge at all times. If it was not the director, then it needed to be the assistant director or even someone else whose name was listed on the wall in case the licensing bureau came out and needed to talk with someone in charge, or if there was some sort of emergency. I remember how hard it was hiring responsible people to take on that role. It seemed like our education was concentrating on emergencies. Staff would not come to work consistently, and it was hard to get satisfactory substitute teachers. We were burglarized, and the person who opened the facility made the discovery.

The burglars took all the computers and cameras. It was hard for a long time to count on someone to open the childcare center. One time an employee opened and called me, saying, "Mr. Bill, I've got an emergency. I gotta leave." I got there as fast as I could and discovered the employee had left water running in our "pantry bathroom," where the food was stored. Education is not without its frustrations. I learned how to pinch pennies and be frugal too. For example, our milk delivery man charged a lot. So, I started stopping at Walmart and purchasing the milk myself, which saved us more than half of what we had been charged.

How did we wind up with a second childcare center despite all these problems and challenges? Another friend of Ellen's planted the seed. At around the time we were running GEMS 1, he was a Fulton County school bus driver. While driving one day to his schools, he saw some land next door to a school that was "zoned for childcare." It was all woods. He talked with us, and like most married business partners, we discussed it, and we discussed it, and we discussed it.

Ellen suggested I go down to St. Simons Island "until you can have it resolved; can we do it or can't we?" I stayed in St. Simon's for four days and thoroughly enjoyed myself. I loved the beach. I had grown up around it. I thought about a second daycare center during the day while relaxing on the beach, then at night I would leave the beach and go to work on my legal pad. At three one morning, it came to me: "We can do it," I told Ellen on the phone. So, I left the beach and came back home to meet a fresh new challenge.

We decided to contact the people who had the land. We put down a deposit to hold the land contingent upon getting a loan from a bank for a childcare center. However, we were not able to get loan in time for the deadline. We lost that money. The second time we put money up for thirty days, we applied to one of the outstanding banks in Atlanta. They thought the business plan was great and suggested we take it to Clayton

State University's business incubator. We then went on a ten-day cruise. When we returned to GEMS 1, we saw all the mail, including a letter from the bank. Our thinking was it would be good news, but they had rejected us and our plan for getting the land. We got another builder who had not wanted us to go to that bank in the first place and was going to build a bigger childcare center. The third time we went to the landowners, they wanted a down payment. We went to builder number two with our funding dilemma. This was a truly frustrating process and a costly one. Builder two said he would put the money up for us and motivated us to apply to his bank. We got it! I remember that it cost $40,000 just to reroute the school's water that was draining on our property from next door. We sent his bank the same business plan. They loved it and could not believe anyone else had turned it down.

With a second childcare center came double the costly education that Dock McQueen had told me about. We hired a marketing company in California; they shamed us. But we did not quit. We went around to the surrounding neighborhood and put flyers in mailboxes announcing our new childcare center. This was wrong on our part. It was okay to tape notices to the mailbox but not to put them in the boxes, which is against the law. We received a letter from the postmaster saying we had to stop or they would fine us or put us in jail. We found a Georgia company that was legitimate. We did marketing mailers two times a year, in March and July. Each time, I promised a huge deal of four weeks of free childcare but used the small print with parameters on the four weeks free, stating that the deal was only in place if the parents or guardians applied using the mailed card. We also paid a marketing company to monitor the incoming telephone calls and had the receptionists complete a card on each new family that inquired about GEM childcare services.

Another lesson came from having to borrow money from the builder for utilities. Marketing was key and critical, and we paid him back when we broke even in May/June. This was contrary to what he believed based on his experience in constructing childcare centers, which was his specialty.

There was no Georgia pre-K program at GEMS 2, just at GEMS 1. There were no more programs to give out, but they could transfer GEMS 1's program to GEMS 2. We held the graduation from GEMS 1's pre-K at GEMS 2. Then the next year, they moved the Georgia pre-K program over to GEMS 2. At that time pre-K teachers did not need a degree. We had a problem keeping to standards of the Georgia pre-K program. Our family friend (Ellen's "brother") revealed his special, special skills with the Georgia pre-K manual he created. The evaluator from Georgia pre-K saw the manual he had created and was flabbergasted. She wanted to take the forms from that manual.

A gentler "lesson" came from an experience that I always wanted to apply to the management of our staff but was prevented from doing so. That was how different it is if you know somebody and you know their skills and you can get what you want and what you need. Count on them and praise them. I was blocked from doing this to the full extent that I wanted to because "some people won't accept that they can't do everything well." Enough said.

GEMS 2 also had legal problems. The first lawsuit involved a situation where two little boys went into the bathroom at the same time and one of them touched the other. At the time it happened, the teacher was talking across the hall to another teacher. There were not supposed to be two children in the bathroom at the same time, although there were no cameras in the bathroom. The children had just come out of the pool. After spending a week in court and being called to take the stand twice, we lost the case and it cost the insurance company $500,000. That insurance company stopped insuring GEMS 2, and we had to get another insurance company, which cost a lot more each year.

The next major legal battle came when I went to court without a lawyer. This problem came from our earliest three-year-old class. The grandmother of a child in that classroom came to pick him up. He had been sleeping a lot. His grandmother took him to the hospital. All the mom wanted me to do was pay for the hospital's seven or eight hundred dollar bill. "I'll take you to court!" she swore. "See you in court, then!" I vowed. I told the judge what happened, and the judge said, "Don't say another word: pay the plaintiff fifteen thousand dollars." I had the money and paid after exploring how expensive it would be to fight the fine in regards to lawyers, fees, and time. But I believe the man upstairs handles things, and one day that mother will get what is coming to her.

We were not always successful in the child-care business. One significantly challenging period was 2008 to 2010, when it was tough paying bills. Taxes were not built into the regular payments. We had three loans: SBA (Small Business Association), PNC, Zions Bank (the builder's bank). I continued to pay the note but put paying the taxes off. I kept telling myself, "I'll pay them later, I'll pay them later." Zions needed to know what I was planning on doing regarding paying my property taxes. If I did not respond and pay, they would put our building up for sale to get the taxes. I did not know what to do. I creatively considered how to finance this expense. I asked the SBA to reduce my monthly payment and allow me to pay my taxes over time. The SBA agreed. Zions Bank did not agree. The loan officer said, "We have the first mortgage. We can sell your building and get taxes and mortgage. We need to collect more information to consider your proposal." Every time I sent them more information, they would ask for more. But within a month's time, I had the money to pay the taxes. I called Zions with the news. The Zions loan officer said, "Okay, we'll reduce your payment. Don't pay the taxes; they'll be paid by us." This was a miracle, but an even greater miracle was what I told them that day: "Thank you, but I figured out a way to pay my taxes, and I'll send you the receipt. Leave the agreement the way it is, and I'll pay the taxes and the note. And by the way, what is your boss's name? I want to write to your boss about how you helped me to do better." SBA reduced the loan for a year, then it went back up.

After many years in the childcare business, my wife and I decided to retire. In October 2016 we sold the childcare center and made a significant profit. All in all, it took a lot out of me, but it was a good experience overall. If it had not happened, I probably still wouldn't be around. I had a longtime desire to create and develop my own business, so it was a dream come true. I did a lot of things myself instead of outsourcing them because I wanted to learn how to do them.

To be the best was my goal, and that meant being better than anything else out there. I also saw this business as another offshoot of social work for systemic change. I wanted to improve the staff's capability to work with children and parents. I wanted to demonstrate that I could borrow a large sum of money for a business investment as a Black man. During that time a first-class Black childcare center was not present within a five-mile radius. This was considered a low-income area, and I wanted that to change.

Nobody knows the ups and downs and fears and rewards of being in business for yourself until you have gone through it. Planning, financing, building, operating and managing GEMS II, our second child care facility, tested my beliefs, education, experience, knowledge, skill, patience, and dreams. I like to think that because of us at GEMS II and the stellar service we provided, we changed for the better the child care business environment as a small "mom and pop" business that was the backbone of our vision and an outstanding version of the American Dream.

From dirt to brick and mortar, we created something from nothing: a state of the art child care facility the likes of which our mostly African-American, although of mixed socio-economic background, clientele had never seen before. We were doing something new and unique and sometimes faking it until we made it. The learning curve was steep. GEMS II was our precious stone, a foundation for success in the local community, and our entrepreneurial bedrock of unprecedented, non-franchise wealth. Every risk we took was calculated, but I believe we were also greatly blessed. We wanted to make the kind of child care center that we would have felt comfortable leaving our children and grandchildren at, had we needed it. We did not just offer child care services, we enabled the children's family to have the peace of mind that comes from knowing one's children are safe and clean while learning academics and social skills so that their loved ones could focus on earning a living to pay for it, free from worry.

Let's first consider the factors that made the facility great. The building's capacity was for 12 classrooms. Our license was for 216 children but would expand to 246 in order to accommodate the children from the six feeder schools we served and picked up from with our after-school program. We ran two buses and two vans in order to operate this program. One of these schools was right next door.

We built children's self-esteem, empowered their confidence, and promoted their emotional growth by naming each of GEMS II's classrooms after a gem. We felt that each child that received care there was as dear and valuable as a rare gem. We had: pearl, topaz, emerald, turquoise, amber, aquamarine, garnet, amethyst, jasper, diamond, sapphire and jade. (If we would have had another classroom, we would have named it "ruby", after my mother-in-law's name, even though we all affectionately called her "Sweet Mama". She lived to see it come to fruition and came to the center to bless it with an ancestor's blessing.). We also provided solid and stable employment for 26 employees.

We were not without problems, however. But we kept our business functioning in the face of a recession, survived constant challenges with collecting from children's parents or guardians for the services we provided, and dealt with high turnover by becoming adept at keeping fully staffed and in compliance at all times as best practices or in case of a surprise visit from the state licensing agency. Nevertheless, through it all, my wife was the "mom" and I was the "pop" and we made our business consistently thrive for 15 years against all the odds and despite our advanced age. Somehow we made it and made a difference.

Why not you?

1. Are you willing to sacrifice everything—savings, investments, house note—for a personal goal, dream, or vision?

2. Are you striving to be the best in any area or goal?

3. Do you want to be an entrepreneur?

4. Do you have what it takes to survive and thrive as an entrepreneur?

5. Do you think you would be able to last more than three to five years in a new business you owned?

6. Could you survive an economic downturn or recession that could force a business to close?

7. Are you considering a partnership or a sole proprietorship, and what are the advantages and disadvantages of each for your business's ability to succeed and survive?

8. Would you have a for-profit or a not-for-profit business?

Conclusions

Full retirement is the current season of my life after many years as a high achiever. I am now living a goal-free life, where my go-getter time now has been replaced by reminiscing and socializing with family and friends, giving advice, and interacting with all of the people who made up my pre retirement years. For you, however, things could just be getting started, and you could be at the beginning of your story.

I am grateful for the life I have lived. I have never been without a job. I am still healthy. I have been blessed to only miss a short period of work. I am simply an ordinary man with some extraordinary life experiences. The mentors in my life

have guided me to success. My first wife sacri-
ficed a lot; my second wife carried the torch of
hope for success in a transitional part of my life. I
have always worked toward a vision. I have been
open to mentors when their wisdom truly count-
ed and benefited me. I give the air force credit for
my wanting to get educated. Most importantly,
God has been my ultimate mentor and guide. He
is the chief reason why all of the moments of success have happened. It is to him I give the glory
and him I celebrate.

I may not have all the answers, but I hope
that my story will put someone on track to finding solutions that match their needs and maybe
some of their wants. Stay focused, be prepared
to go on your own growth journey filled with its
own growing pains, but come out the other end
ready to bless the world with the contributions
that only you can make. Remember, my story is
my journey. It is meant to be instructive, not lim-
iting. It is meant to be inspirational, not boastful.
It is meant to show you that if I could do it, then
you can too.

I believe that who you want to become is only limited by who you think you can become. I believe that if you seek to help others, somehow your potential to succeed broadens. If you focus yourself on a life of success defined by helping others, you will become an individual who accepts nothing less than your personal best, leaving your mark behind wherever you go. Why shouldn't you progress from ordinary to extraordinary and live to make a contribution that makes a difference in your own life and in those of others? That is the legacy that I leave after the life I have led. May your examination of the way I've lived guide you toward being a self-defined success and may this little life guide lead you to ask, "Why not me?" I hope my life story will help you to unleash your potential and discover who you are, to unlock who you can become, and to liberate the contribution that only you can make, which will lead you to your destiny.

I am the first to admit that my story was not always linear. Now, looking back over the course of my life and evaluating the different moments

I lived through and the diverse accomplishments that I have enjoyed, I truly feel that I made a difference. That is what I want for you: the legacy of a life well lived so that people will know that you have made your mark on your community, your job(s), your friends, and your family. I want you to write your spiritual signature on the hearts, minds, and souls of everyone you have interacted with. Whether they had an effect on you or you on them, it is equal, because chances are you are already living and leaving a legacy behind.

My story is not the golden nugget. Your story of answering profound questions about yourself is the true treasure. I see my story as the treasure map that may help you to start to find out "Why not you?" and embark on a journey of personal discovery that will lead you to personal success in whichever direction you decide to go. When you choose your path, may you contribute based on the unique gift that you are, and may the success you become have no limitations except those that you impose. Just remember that wherever you are, there is always something you can do, and there is still a contribution that you can make and feel good about.

Ultimately, it is my wish that you continue to live in an even better, more deliberate way, examining your course as you move forward. I pray that you can confirm you are living your dreams and getting on a track to align yourself with your destiny. I hope you are building meaningful moments by looking forward to what you want to achieve and reflecting proudly on what you have already done, remarking on the significant number of people you have interacted with and influenced. Then you will be ready to meet your maker someday and have him say, "Well done!"

Acknowledgements

There are a number of persons that I owe a debt of gratitude for assisting me in bringing this project to fruition. First and foremost I must thank my wife, *Ellen Wade McQueen,* for the support and encouragement she has given during the many hours I spent drafting my thoughts.

This would have also been impossible had I not had the love and support of my daughter, *April D. McQueen*, who interviewed me and captured much of what is recorded herein. Her skills and talents as a gifted writer are most appreciated.

Dr. Robert R. Jennings is owed a world of thanks for not only editing this volume but for helping me to restructure and clarify many of my thoughts. Also, there are a number of other friends and colleagues who encouraged, inspired and motivated me during those moments when I felt like quitting. Among them are the late *A. W. Haywood* and his lovely wife, *Alma Haywood, Evelyn Hughes* and my cousin's son, *Ronald Phillips, Robin D. Woodyard.* Thank you for all your love and support during this book journey.

To God be the glory for all of your kindness!